The HEALING
ENERGIES
OF MUSIC

QUEST BOOKS
are published by
The Theosophical Society in America
a branch of a world organization
dedicated to the promotion of brotherhood and
the encouragement of the study of religion,
philosophy, and science, to the end that man may
better understand himself and his place in
the universe. The Society stands for complete
freedom of individual search and belief.
In the Theosophical Classics Series
well-known occult works are made
available in popular editions.

Cover design by Pamela Preciado
The painting on the cover is by Jonathan Wiltshire.
It represents the thought form created by the finale of
Rachmaninoff's Piano Concerto Number 2.

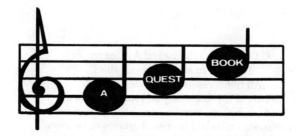

The HEALING ENERGIES OF MUSIC

Hal A. LINGERMAN

*This publication made possible with
the assistance of the Kern Foundation*

The Theosophical Publishing House
Wheaton, Ill. U.S.A.
Madras, India/London, England

© Copyright 1983 by Hal A. Lingerman
Fourth Printing, Revised, 1988
All rights reserved. A Quest original
No part of this book may be reproduced in any
manner without written permission except for
quotations embodied in critical articles or reviews.
For additional information write to:
The Theosophical Publishing House, 306 West Geneva Road,
Wheaton, Illinois 60187.
Published by the Theosophical Publishing House,
a department of the Theosophical Society in America

Library of Congress Cataloging in Publication Data

Lingerman, Hal A., 1943 -
The healing energies of music.

"A Quest original."
Bibliography: p.
Includes index.
1. Music therapy.   I. Title.
ML3920.L695   1983   615.8'5154   82-42706
ISBN 0-8356-0570-1 (pbk.)

Printed in the United States of America

Contents

Preface   vii

Introduction   1

Chapter

1. Music for You—A Closer Relationship   9

2. Music for Better Health and Well-Being   13

3. Finding Your Music   38

4. Music for Daily Life   62

5. Music for Home and Family   68

6. The Music of Nature   86

7. Angelic Music   99

8. Music to God and the Christ   106

9. A Gallery of Great Composers   114

10. The Deeper Mysteries of Music   139

11. Music for the Future   145

Appendix A

   Music for Stress Reduction, Relaxation and Focus 150

Appendix B

   1. Chiefly Classical Masterpieces 151

   2. Lighter Selections 173

   3. Christmas Music 182

   4. An Easter Program 184

   5. Music for Nature and the Four Seasons 186

   6. Additional Children's Music 189

Bibliography 191

Index 195

Preface

I value the transforming power of beautiful MUSIC! I am deeply indebted to music for the way it enriches my life. Music is far more than a source of entertainment; it is a vital food which nourishes me daily. I believe great music, carefully selected and experienced, is a unique agent for healing, attunement, inspiration and expanded spiritual consciousness.

I am professionally trained as a minister, counselor and teacher. In each of these professions music helps and inspires me in ways that are both obvious and subtle. Whatever I have felt and learned about music through the years, I have shared daily with others, as environment and appropriate timing have allowed. The results have been gratifying, as I have observed improvement in others' physical health, emotional stability, mental focus and spiritual sensitivity. Many times I have seen how beautiful music can contribute toward balance in the personality, peace in the psyche and enpowerment from the soul within and the Infinite beyond ourselves.

In this book I am sharing with you some of the insights that have come to me through great music. My approach is *synthesis*: it cuts across various fields, such as history and biography, psychology, philosophy, science, medicine, religion, metaphysics and esoteric studies. In my own life and in my love of music I have been led to follow a more mystical path. During my years in the ministry, I have moved through orthodox, metaphysical and esoteric groups, finding truth in all places. I believe strongly in the teaching of reincarnation, the existence of beings in nature who work through inner dimensions of life, the great reality of Angels, and the abiding divine Presence as the inspiration for this earth's humanity. I also acknowledge God's helpers, both visible and invisible, with whom we are linked in Light, as we serve the cause of the highest that we know.

Years of spiritual seeking behind the literal or academic view of things have only confirmed my conviction that Truth is far deeper and more subtle than any one literal approach or interpretation. We are instructed: "By their fruits ye shall know them." One's life is larger than one's beliefs: whatever path we follow, life will demand increasing purity—of mind, emotions and body. Disharmony or imbalance on any level of consciousness produces fear and stress within the personality, and, if not dealt with, will eventually lead to frustration, dis-ease, illness.

Today we live in a time of history that is dynamic and filled with rapid changes. Many persons are feeling a hunger that is spiritual as well as material. Internal and external growing pains in mankind are demanding serious questioning of former ideas, systems and assumptions. New energies and seeds of thought are leading individuals into new evidence that this planet, as part of God's cosmos, is far greater and more magnificently integrated into the universal life-direction than we can grasp with our five senses. We are now developing higher senses of intuition and insight that will lead us into the future and the coming Aquarian Age of increased brotherhood and loving good will.

There are those today who are taking a pessimistic and fatalistic view of mankind's future. I prefer to see our times as a dynamic opportunity for individual and planetary transformation. Now is the time to dig in, get involved, and work for a cause greater than one's own pleasure or self-interest. Enough individuals, working together in networks of Light and prayer-filled activity, will make a huge difference in the future of mankind's destiny. Every life of service and source of good will can help to bring about a new cleansing and a more healthy direction.

I believe music can be one such catalyst for good. Music is an extremely important instrument of the Divine. When it is used wisely and effectively, music will attune man to higher sources of love and power, thus strengthening his character and goals, and giving him increased spiritual purpose on earth.

I wish to thank many friends who have helped me and inspired me to write this book: in particular, my mother and father, who always encouraged my love of music, Paul M. and Paul G. Traudl, Marge and Elden, Stan, Elsie, Lynn, Dr. Dika Newlin, Jerrie, Ken, Trudy, Helen, Walter, Lucy, Joy, Clare and Ben. I'm very grateful to Rosemary, my wonderful wife, whose kindness and loving friendship enrich my life each day; and I thank the Reverend Flower A. Newhouse, spiritual teacher and Christian mystic, whose sensitivity to music and nature has provided me with many valuable insights, some of which appear in this book. Finally, my gratitude to Jonathan Wiltshire, artist and friend, whose painting reproduced on the cover has added so much; and thanks to Dr. John Diamond, whose book, *Your Body Doesn't Lie*, has confirmed so many of my own findings. I also wish to thank Dr. Karl Haas, who has inspired me greatly with his illuminating radio series on music of the great composers.

The powers that can be communicated to earth by means of music are as yet scarcely suspected by the average individual.

But the time is fast approaching when Man will select his music with the same intelligent care and knowledge he now uses to select his food. When that time comes, music will become a principal source of healing for many individual and social ills, and human evolution will be tremendously accelerated.

Corrine Heline, *Esoteric Music*

*That music always round me,
   unceasing, unbeginning—
yet long untaught I did
   not hear;
But now the chorus I hear
   and am elated;...
I hear not the volumes of sound
   merely—I am
   moved by the exquisite meanings,
I listen to the different voices
   winding in and out,
...now I think I begin
to know them.*

Walt Whitman, *Leaves of Grass*

Introduction

Music is the universal language.
Richard Wagner

Sound and Light influence every area of life. How we respond to these two great universal forces will condition a large part of our health and happiness. It is, therefore, essential to learn how to use sound and light more wisely, so that their energies can flow into us and our environment, filling life with joy, vitality and clear direction.

We live in *music*! The universe is a tonal harmony of many sounds—many lives interacting and vibrating together as they fill the great silence. Your life either contributes to this creative harmony, or it produces a discord. You either make music or noise. Music is the positive pole of sound; its rhythms and melodies echo the eternal harmonies of the heavens. In this way music is a mirror of holy resonance: it opens transparencies in us, enlarging our horizons and helping us to feel what is beautiful and inspiring. Great music nourishes us. It is always strengthening, because it attunes us to powerful waves of life energy and to the unfathomable Source of all Good.

Noise is the opposite of music: it is "sound gone crazy," for its insanity is really its disconnectedness—its failure to find any agreement or harmony with the universe in which

1

it is moving. Great music resolves chaos dynamically, bringing peace, beauty, synthesis and transformation; noise emphasizes separation, ugliness and distortion. Depending upon our own deepest desires and sensitivity, we will choose the sounds best for us.

Stories come down to us about how sensitive and skilled the ancients were in using music as a healing art. For them music was not just a form of entertainment; it was also a source of health, containing chords of rhythm and melody that harmonize and re-balance the human organism, draining away its impurities. We learn from Manly Hall, prolific writer on esoteric traditions, of an incident in ancient Greece, when an angry man charged an enemy, sword drawn, ready to kill. Suddenly "a wise Pythagorean," sensing the situation, struck one chord on his lyre. Instantly, all anger and hatred were drawn out of the would-be attacker and he became gentle as a lamb.

Pythagoras of Samos, a very wise teacher of ancient Greece, knew how to work with sound. He taught his students how certain musical chords and melodies produce definite responses within the human organism. He demonstrated that the right sequence of sounds, played musically on an instrument, can change behavior patterns and accelerate the healing process.

In the Old Testament we also read about the power and therapeutic value of beautiful music. Saul, an ancient king, was troubled "by an evil spirit." He was advised as follows:

> ...seek out a man, who is a wise player on a harp:
> and it shall come to pass,...that he shall play with
> his hand and thou shalt be well.
>
> I Samuel 16:16

Saul sent for David, whom he "found favorable in his sight," and when David played his lyre for the king, these were the results:

...David took a harp, and played with his hand: and Saul was refreshed, and was well, and the evil spirit departed from him.

I Samuel 16:23

From these examples, it is clear that the ancients sensed the power and value of beautiful music, and they knew how to use it to promote harmony and well-being in their lives. Likewise, today we can rediscover the therapeutic and spiritual potencies of great music.

In my work as teacher, counselor and minister, I have been able to observe many situations where music has been a powerful factor for change and improvement in conditions. Certain pieces of music, played with timing and good taste, have helped to deepen understanding and communication in many relationships. These musical selections, sounding through persons, have helped to alter heartbeat and nervous system favorably, and they have promoted greater relaxation, more constructive attitudes and a willingness to listen and be receptive to new directions. I have also observed how specific musical selections contribute in changing attunement, behavior and productivity. I remember several patients in nursing homes who sat inert and unresponsive in their seats until a certain piece of music played through them. They then suddenly began to move, to clap their hands, to smile, hum, sing, talk with each other, and keep time with their feet. A single piece of music, carefully played, can alter the entire atmosphere and behavior in a place. Dr. John Diamond, a well-known medical doctor and researcher into the powerful factor of music in our lives, demonstrated this fact in his book, *Your Body Doesn't Lie* (pp. 103-104).

One factory in particular, a manufacturing and repair plant for sophisticated electronic equipment, where concentration and clear-headedness are essential, was playing a great deal of rock on its continual music broadcast system. It was recommended that this be eliminated. The management changed to different music and found to their delight an immediate increase in productivity and an equally pleasing decrease in errors, even though the employees were quite vocal about their dissatisfaction at having had their favorite music removed.

These experiences and others like them have immense value for our lives. They speak to our times of stress and challenge and point the way to a rediscovery of the healing energies of great music and how we can use music to increase harmony and clarity in our working environment, our homes, our leisure and wherever we may be. I use the word healing to suggest balance and integration of all the ingredients of the personality. Music, wisely used, can help to bring clearance and purification to the body, emotions and thinking patterns within the personality. Music can also open the listener to deeper spiritual dimensions of strength within and around him.

This book is written to help you to discover great music and how to draw upon its powerful, integrating currents, so that your life can find deeper creative attunement with the healing reservoirs of sound and light that direct this universe.

I have found that great music is always inspired. In its own way it is immortal; its unique essence overrides personal tastes and preferences, so that it pours through listeners like a life fluid, gaining access and opening doors where all else has failed. Often great music influences persons therapeutically, despite previous conditioning, opinions or experiences. Finally, music that is truly immortal, that is greater than its particular style or the historical period in which it was composed, transmits an abiding essence which speaks to every generation.

I remember playing certain musical selections for a friend several years ago in New Jersey. When he heard this music for the first, and even the tenth time, he ridiculed it. He said he found it "weird, far out and too different." Subliminally, however, he must have found it intriguing as it triggered strong emotional responses in him. He soon returned and asked for more of "that strange stuff." I obliged. Gradually, he became fascinated by the sounds of the symphony orchestra, with many melodies interweaving. He was captivated by the colors and sonorities of different instruments all blending together. He responded particularly to the strings and powerful crescendos of brass and timpani. I noticed that he was concentrating and really giving himself to the music for the first time. Whereas previously he had paced up and down in the room, talking nervously, he now chose to sit down. His breathing changed, and he became more introspective—even meditative. By the end of that year he had bought more than two hundred new recordings, most of them containing "that weird stuff." Later, he wrote to me, telling me how some pieces of music had inspired him to write a book of poetry. He mentioned to me how different he felt: "...more connected and centered—more interested in things." I noticed he had become more purposeful in his job, and how much more carefully he chose his working environment. The nourishing power of the music he found overrode all previous experiences and tastes. It awakened a deeper layer in him and affected his responses to daily ups and downs. It increased attunement to his own life path. Today great music still nourishes him.

The highest purpose in life is to live completely in conscious union with God. The more we cultivate great music in our lives, the greater will be our attunement to unlimited sources of the Creator's power and direction. Such music will strengthen us to define and accomplish our earthly goals. Develop a deeper friendship with great music, and you will see many areas of your life begin to open. Here are examples of what music can do:

Increase physical vitality, relieve fatigue and inertia.
Pierce through moods, calm anxiety and tensions, uplift feelings.
Focus thinking, clarify goals, release courage and follow-through.
Deepen relationships, enrich friendships.
Stimulate creativity and sensitivity.
Strengthen character and constructive behavior.
Expand consciousness of God and horizons of spiritual attunement.

We were all created equal, but we are born into each lifetime with different temperaments, personalities and inclinations to harmonize. Learning to choose our path with discernment and sharing with each other, we move toward fuller expression of the Divine Presence, filling our personhood. Often we may feel the Light at the center of us and beyond us, which fills our blind spots and rights our imbalances. Particular pieces of great music, pouring their healing energies through us, help to emphasize Light; they remind us to focus on the best in ourselves, which is of God, while we attend to those areas that need correction and overcoming. Seek out music that increases your wellbeing and transforms ugliness and chaos. Music can lead you into activities and horizons of consciousness that are beautiful as your greatest dreams and life goals.

I have included an extended annotated appendix to give added descriptions and suggestions for music that is therapeutic. These listings include the composer, conductor or soloist, and the label number for the recording that has helped me the most. These suggestions for particular interpretations are the results of more than twenty years of careful research. With these references, you will also be able to locate each piece of music more easily, knowing how to look for it in libraries, record shops or tape dealers. For further study and insight, learn to use a

Schwann Record-Tape Catalogue, which announces new recordings each month. If a recording listed here is not listed in the current catalogue, you can still use the number and label to locate this particular interpretation through your dealer. Compare different recordings of the same musical work to find the energies, shadings and interpretations that benefit you most. Refer also to the Musical Heritage Society catalog (14 Park Rd., Tinton Falls, N.J. 07724).

1

Music and You—
A Closer Relationship

> *Each time we listen to beautiful music, we select an impression to weave into the harmony of our unfoldment.*
>
> F. A. Newhouse

How deeply do you feel music? How much of yourself do you give? The more you can give of yourself to the music you are experiencing, the more energy vibrations of power will sound through you. If you come to great music with an open heart, a willing mind and a relaxed body, it will enter you and renew you. Great music brings healing streams and electrical chargings, but these cannot enter and revitalize you if you are distracted, tense and resistant, critical, impatient, ungrateful or poorly prepared.

Because our attunement is faulty and we are scattered, we sometimes miss the finest things in life. A poet has written, "The Angels come to visit us, and we know them only after they are gone." If you take time to prepare yourself beforehand for your music, it will play *through you*, not just around you. You will receive the full power and beauty of great music by learning better how to relax and link with the melodies that you are hearing.

Take a comfortable position, either in your favorite chair (couch), or spread out on the floor. If you are outside, lie down on the grass or relax against a favorite tree. Use these ten keys to prepare yourself for a more meaningful musical experience.

Before Beginning the Music

1. Come to quiet for a minute.

    Speak to your body; tell any tense areas to relax.

    Speak to your feelings; tell them to be calm.

    Speak to your mind; let go of racing thoughts.

    Realize the Divine Presence in whom you will listen.
        You might want to use an affirmation or verse to center yourself, such as "Be still and know that I am God."

    Keep this exercise short, simple and enjoyable.

2. Be grateful for the music you are about to experience. Say "Thank you."

3. Surrender to the music. Try to open yourself to the music you hear.

While the Music is Playing

4. Release all tensions into the music.

    Feel your music pulling you out of all negativity and tension.

    Wherever there is a block in yourself, visualize an opening.

    Breathe deeply, taking in the music. Let go completely.

5. Feel the music embracing and filling you.

    Release all need to dominate or control the situation.

    Open up to the healing, revitalizing currents of melody that are entering you. Go inside the sound.

6. Give yourself to the music. Enjoy the music wherever it takes you.

7. Be filled with joy and praise.

When the Music is Over.

8. Do not play music for too long at a time.

9. Take time to absorb your music. Sit quietly for a few minutes after it has finished.

10. When appropriate, combine musical experiencing with other activity, such as keeping a diary, sketching, dancing or moving, or doing chores such as housework, cooking, or working in the shop.

Even before you hear the first note, it matters greatly *where* you hear your music. Is the setting beautiful? Take the time to cultivate the most advantageous surroundings for your musical experiences. Here are four suggestions to help you:

1. Experience your music in a beautiful place.

   Avoid clutter, heaviness, ugliness and darkness.

   Clear the atmosphere, heighten colors and seek Light.

2. Play your music in a quiet place.

   Minimize outer noise and distractions.

   Turn off T.V., avoid loud hums of electrical appliances.

   Let your music emerge out of quiet, or listen to music in nature. Be sensitive to the sounds of nature—bird calls, rain, woods, streams, wind, ocean—as these combine with musical melodies to uplift you and link you with the Eternal.

   Find the particular volume (loudness) that is best for you.

3. Buy good equipment. Find a stereo or sound system with speakers that play music with a clear tone and

minimal distortion. Choose your equipment carefully and patiently, after hearing some of your favorite recordings played on it. Trust your own ear. Explore many different speaker systems before deciding. Do not buy, necessarily, according to brand name or advertising.

4. Take good care of your system, tapes and recordings. Clean your records when they are dusty. Do not stack your records. Play one record at a time. Clean the tape heads regularly and remove dust from needle, carefully.

For increased therapeutic value, you should not be critical of the music you are experiencing. If you are a fussy listener, you will not soar. The quality of performances and pressings varies. Find recordings you can live with and love them unconditionally for all they have to offer. Emphasize the treasures of the music, not the defects. Listen behind the notes for the overtones, the larger melodies and the archetypes that the composer may have "heard" and partially brought through. Move into the silences between the notes. Such an attitude of openness and gratitude will expand the range and depth of the musical experiences that come to you. In an atmosphere of joyful acceptance, the healing vibrations of great music can better find entrance into you and will bring you the greatest possible enjoyment and upliftment.

Discover the great golden moments in music and arrange them into the most healing and beneficial sequences that will meet your various needs. Use the lists throughout this book and the further suggestions in the appendix to help you find just the right music for you.

NOTE: From thorough scientific research, Dr. John Diamond and others have found that the most recently developed digital recordings (produced from a computer) have not yet proved to be therapeutic. I have no proof of this myself, but from my own work with people I have often found that older non-digital recordings, made from a master tape, have achieved better results.

2

Music for Better Health and Well-Being

The only correct music is that which is beautiful and noble.
Ralph Vaughan Williams

While the greatest pieces of music will energize and inspire all levels of your being, there are different musical works that will appeal specifically to certain areas in your make-up. Some music will primarily affect the physical body. Such pieces might make you feel stronger and more energetic in your movements; other pieces might make you want to move more, perhaps through dancing, house cleaning, painting, or even typing. Other selections will affect the feelings-emotions more. Perhaps a certain tune or song will make you cry, while another will bring out greater devotion, determination or even anger. Still another selection of music will appeal mostly to your mind, inspiring you with a new idea, seed thoughts of clarity and creativity. Finally, there are those pieces of music that penetrate through all outer layers. This kind of music speaks directly to the heart and soul, reminding you of your whole, divine connection and highest selfhood in God.

Different pieces of music stimulate different areas. Melodic music, played by solo instruments and chamber ensembles, is quieting. Such music is usually more soothing than the potencies of full orchestral and choral pieces. Play symphonies, concertos, cantatas and such larger works when you want a greater inpouring bath of musical sound. Cultivate chamber music for intimate, quiet times, when you desire a more calming influence. As a general rule, different instruments affect particular parts of your make-up, as follows:

1. Physical Body—brass, percussion, heavy sounds of bass notes; electronic music (most of it).
2. Emotional—woodwinds and strings
3. Mental—strings
4. Soul—harp and organ; wind chimes; high strings.

Seek out the kind of music you need to balance and awaken all of you. Discover the times and sequences in which a certain musical selection is most appropriate.

MUSIC FOR THE PHYSICAL BODY

The physical body is the earthly temple for the soul. It is important to love and care for your physical body in every possible way. And as you would seek to feed, clothe, clean, exercise and rest your body wisely, so can you use certain music to bathe, purify and energize this physical vehicle.

Use certain musical selections to pierce through physical inertia and lumpiness; use other musical favorites to sound through hyperactivity and tension, relaxing your nerves and muscles.

If your physical body needs energizing, play music with stronger rhythms, peppy tunes and powerful contrasts. Instrumentally, choose music for piano, or stronger sounds of brass and percussion. Pieces for trumpets, horns, tubas, saxhorns, trombones, timpani, cymbals, and gongs are very powerful. They will ground you very quickly, if you feel you are too lethargic or "spaced out."

However, be careful *never to play this kind of music too much or too long or too loud*. If you overexpose yourself to such powerful sounds, even though they are melodious, you will shock and exhaust yourself very quickly. "Big moments" in music always build up from quietness; mighty crescendos emerge out of silence. The great artist and composer Pablo Casals said that all musical masterpieces are created from the resolution between tension and release. Music that achieves a dynamic reconciliation of opposites will make you feel strong and victorious. Your body will feel better each time you experience music that harmonizes conflicts and dissonances in life with a new musical solution. Avoid continuous blasts of noise and chaos without melody. In the same way, mere pleasant, linear, "blah" music will leave you feeling stale and dull, equally unsatisfied.

Marches. Many marches, composed for orchestra or band, are a healthy stimulus to your physical body. Marches pierce through inertia and defy negativity. They call you to attention and focus, stirring you to clarify your goals and to take decisive action. In a larger way, some marches promote greater cooperation and brotherhood, and they inspire. Marches awaken loyalty and are often a powerful medicine for combating an enemy, either external or within oneself. Here are some suggestions for marches that will inspire and activate your physical body. See the appendix for label numbers and more suggestions.

Pomp and Circumstance, No. 1, by Sir Edward Elgar (Philips 6502001): This great, ennobling piece of music is vivid and very powerful. It lifts you in every area of your being, not just the physical body. It will stir you with energy and desire for group mobilization to achieve common purposes and goals. If played at a memorial service, it will scatter sorrow and depression, making those present feel the value of time and earthly opportunity that are still available to them.

Powerful chords of melody, like beacons of white Light, sound through this music, charging and filling your body with renewed energy. It is a thrilling experience to see and feel the power of unity that occurs each year in London at the last night of the Proms, when many thousands of people sing this tune together to the words of "Land of Hope and Glory."

When you listen to "Pomp and Circumstance," envision the purity of white Light filling you with galvanizing power to build and work for the Good.

Recently, as I played this piece of music in a nursing home in a music therapy class, I noticed several patients in wheelchairs. They had been sitting with heads bowed and bodies inert. Suddenly they stirred in their seats. They looked up with eyes opening wide. As the climax came through the music, I saw many in the room that were now smiling, humming along and keeping time with their hands and feet. The entire atmosphere was changed. The nurses smiled at each other, the spirits of the patients were uplifted, and for some time afterwards their conversations became far more animated. Their faces looked less aimless and more focused. One woman said to me, "Boy, that piece really made me feel powerful again."

Triumphal March (from Aida) by Giuseppe Verdi (DGG 2530549): This dramatic march with its accompanying, exultant chorus brings in great strength and power. It lifts the emotions as well as the body. Its festivity rises to disperse all heaviness. Notice the strong melody throughout and the blaze of trumpets that lift you. Strong rhythms are often repeated in the melody. These accents kindle stronger purpose and constancy in the listener. It reminds us that by facing a challenge bravely, it becomes possible to overcome. As it is written to celebrate the victory of a returning army, so will it stir feelings of triumph in you.

I remember hearing this piece recently in a local record store. Persons browsing through the bins stopped, stood at attention and raised their heads upward with dignity and joy. One man, smiling broadly, began to conduct the march with arms raised. After the chorus mounted toward the final crescendo, everyone applauded. Three persons bought the recording.

Marche Slave, by Peter Ilyich Tchaikovsky (London 21026): Varied rhythms and strong, melodic flavors characterize this festive, explosive music. While some of Tchaikovsky's music contains tints of melancholy and shades of sorrow, this piece is far more dynamic and sweeps the listener along. You can sing this music, and you can march to it. The strong rhythms and powerful brass choirs send trumpeting energies through your body. I defy you to sit still, while you listen to this piece. Enjoy it! Do not play it too often, for it is very powerful.

It is interesting to note that the great maestro Leopold Stokowski conducted this showpiece as the concluding selection at a concert in Royal Festival Hall in London to celebrate the sixtieth anniversary of his first appearance with the London Symphony Orchestra. The recording captures the power and fireworks of the music, and at the conclusion you will hear a great roar go out from the audience.

Other Music to Energize the Physical Body:

Sousa - Stars and Stripes Forever
Sibelius - Alla Marcia (from Karelia Suite)
Schubert - March Militaire
Beethoven - Turkish March (from Ruins of Athens)
Clarke - Trumpet Voluntary
J. Strauss (Sr.) - Radetsky March

Overtures. Overtures in general are peppy and dynamic. They are especially good for activating the physical body. For best results play no more than two or three at one sitting.

  Wagner - Die Meistersinger
  Dvořák - Carnival
  Weber - Euryanthe; Oberon
  J. Strauss - Die Fledermaus
  Mozart - Abduction from the Seraglio; Don
   Giovanni; Magic Flute
  Rossini - William Tell; Silken Ladder
  Mendelssohn - A Midsummer Night's Dream
  Arthur Fiedler - Anthology of marches played by
   the Boston Pops.

These pieces of music are very powerful. Use them wisely and do not play them too loudly, or you will defeat your purpose. Just one of these at a time is plenty.

Fanfares, lively songs, epic soundtracks and dances are also categories of music that will vitalize you with their strong frequencies. Explore the pieces to find those that do the most for you. Most of these selections are very strong, so play one or two at a time, then absorb the power before playing more of this kind of music.

Fanfares. Many of these pieces were composed for royal festivals and celebrations. The strong brass sounds will stimulate the physical body. The majestic trumpets and cymbals will energize you, especially if you are feeling lethargic or tending to feel sorry for yourself. If these pieces prove to be too strong and make you withdrawn or angry, then play lighter music.

  Mouret - Fanfares
  DeLalande - Symphonies for the King's Suppers
  Copland - Fanfare for the Common Man
  Dukas - La Péri

Lively Songs. A class that I worked with discussed the kind of music that made them feel recharged and physically renewed. They preferred lively, popular pieces that were often peppy and happy. They also pointed out that they like music with perky rhythms. Here are some of the pieces and performers they liked the most:

A Cockeyed Optimist - South Pacific
Oh, What a Beautiful Morning - Oklahoma
Anderson - Bugler's Holiday
  Syncopated Clock
  Typewriter
Liberace
Johnny Cash

I remember an evening with a dear friend, when we listened together to the beautiful, enlivening melodies of *Brigadoon*. At the end of the performance, my friend said, "I always feel so good after seeing a musical like this; it makes me feel so lively."

In a similar way I notice with interest how one contemporary church group uses as its opening "hymn" the tune to "Oh, What a Beautiful Morning" from *Oklahoma*. Although they have changed the words to fit their religious philosophy, they have picked up on the charging energies. The music brings through energies that lift and stimulate the people with feelings of expectancy that last for the entire service.

Epic Soundtracks. Have you noticed how certain musical soundtracks add so much to the physical and emotional action going on in the scenes? Some of the strong soundtracks from the great motion picture epics wil lead to physical renewal and greater vitality. You will find that, even though you cannot remember the exact scene during which the music was played, the music will galvanize your body. Sometimes it is not even necessary to see the movie; just the recording of the music, itself, is enough to charge you. Here are some of these soundtracks, which happen to be personal favorites of mine:

Ben Hur	Born Free
Superman	Caravans
Empire Strikes Back	Star Wars
E.T.	

When you play these soundtracks, notice the particular bands on each record that appeal to you the most. With soundtrack recordings, there is usually a wide range of musical moods and content. In general, you will find that the main theme (usually first and last bands of the record) is the strongest and often the most memorable.

Dances and Songs from Broadway Shows. Certain music makes you want to dance. The best music of this kind restores your physical body; it does not jar you nor deplete your energies nor make you feel scattered and frenzied. Folk dances and other pieces of beautiful dance music are far different from disco or rock, where wiggling hips and navels are often the main attraction. Just as Zorba the Greek points out that life itself is a dance, so beautiful dance music puts you in touch with all your energy as it flows through you, helping you to feel genuine intimacy in close physical contact and movement with another person. Dancing gracefully and with vitality to a song or melody is a way to share with one you feel close to, and it enables you to touch and embrace the other in an affectionate, wholesome way.

Also, such music provides you with an uplifting form of exercise; it clears out staleness in your emotions, limbs and muscles, and it helps you to breathe new air throughout lungs and bloodstream.

Here are some musical selections of beautiful and lively music:

        Dvořák - Slavonic Dances
        Brahms - Hungarian Dances
        Weber - Invitation to the Dance
        Tchaikovsky - Dances from Swan Lake
            and Sleeping Beauty
        Shostakovich - Polka (from Age of Gold)
        Delibes - Coppelia
        Copland - Rodeo

The appendix includes more suggestions for all these categories, along with label numbers for recommended recordings.

MUSIC FOR FEELINGS AND MOODS

The most challenging area in your make-up is your emotions. Just as the physical body releases energy through movement and activity, the emotions give out energy through the expression of feelings. One of the most important aspects of a balanced and creative life is a healthy, happy and constructive emotional nature.

We usually feel before thinking. Observe your emotional reactions. If something happens that makes you feel happy, how do you express this feeling? Do you sing, do you cry out in joy, do you speak out, do you show happiness by moving your body—by running, hopping, smiling, hugging, or some other way? Pay close attention to your responses to feelings of joy, anger, fear, sadness, tenseness, confusion, guilt, and so forth. How do you release your emotions?

The key to a healthy emotional nature is beautiful expression, not repression, of your feelings. Creative expression and balance of your emotions take time and careful attention, especially if you have repressed your feelings for many years.

Recently, a friend was told, "You are so angry! Why are you so filled with anger?" My friend answered that he was not angry *at anyone* that he could think of. "No," he was reminded, "you are just filled with anger—the stored-up feelings of old anger that were never expressed."

My friend went home and considered carefully what he had been told. He discovered many memories of times when he had felt very angry toward certain persons, but either out of propriety, good manners, or fear, he had swallowed his anger, thus building tightness in his head and solar plexus which had increased with the years and each new instance of turning his angry feelings inside himself. It took my friend a long time to begin to work through the anger and frustration he had stored up. During this process he discovered deep memories of situations when he had wanted to respond emotionally, but instead had just choked back his feelings and repressed the situation. I remember when he finally got in touch with his deep emotion, he said, "If I had gone on like this, some day I might have killed somebody."

You cannot deny nor repress your feelings. If you do, you may eventually become very violent and destructive or melancholic and filled with sadness. Repressed anger turns to sadness or explodes violently, leaving weakness, while creative release of positive and negative emotions brings catharsis and clearance, and leaves you feeling strong and vital.

Healthwise, repressed anger may lead to ulcers, strokes or tumors; prolonged fears may make one tense and may bring on eczema, shingles, psoriasis and arthritis. It is essential, therefore, to find many outlets and creative ways through which to channel emotions. Your daily diet—of food, mental attitudes and spiritual devotion and study—must be supplemented by emotionally rewarding and satisfying interests. Great music is one source of healthy, beautiful emotional release.

You can release emotions creatively through music. The creative arts offer you a wonderful opportunity to transmute negative, suppressed emotional energies. Use artistic outlets like singing, painting, dancing, movement with music, working with clay, writing poetry, keeping a journal to channel the energies and pockets of feeling that are alive in you. And, let music come into you, music that will stir you and at the same time will act as a clearing agent that will take and absorb the feelings you release into it.

You can also clear out emotional blockage with music. I have found generally that music for woodwinds will help clear out emotional tensions and blockage. Light, transparent sounds of the flute, piccolo, oboe, English horn (really an alto oboe), clarinet and sometimes the bassoon, if they play beautiful, melodic music, are wonderful healing agents for strained emotions.

I remember playing a recording of Jean-Pierre Rampal's arrangement for flute of Debussy's *Clair de lune* to a group of rather angry and tense listeners. Shortly, their looks changed. The music was pulling the strain out of them. As this piece bathed them with fountains of effervescent melody, they began to relax. The fighting mood of the group changed, and soon some smiles appeared on their faces. One listener offered the woman next to him a cigarette, which she gratefully accepted. After the music session had ended, the business meeting proceeded much more smoothly, and an attitude of coopertion prevailed.

Sometimes woodwinds are combined with strings to provide a different healing environment and sound texture. A striking example of a piece of this type is the Adagio, 3rd Movement, of Rachmaninoff's Second Symphony. In this marvelously uplifting and therapeutic musical movement, the clarinet leads and carries the melody. The tune is quiet but soars with the full orchestra into great heights. To hear this music is to feel all emotional negativity and tension being drained away. This music not only absorbs the energies you release into it, but in addition it carries you into a higher, deeply devotional state of consciousness. It is one of the greatest works that Rachmaninoff was ever inspired to compose. The movement comes full circle to close in quietness.

Releasing Anger. Music can also be used to release anger. Anger is the name we use to describe one kind of emotional displeasure. When a person feels "angry," it is essential for him to find some way to express this emotion constructively, so that he doesn't swallow it or project it negatively on someone else. Depending upon what kind of person and temperament you are, you will have to find the most appropriate ways to defuse and discharge your anger. Perhaps you will go outside and chop wood; or you might begin to beat the rugs, jog, scrub floors, sing loudly, ride your motorcycle, play racquetball, or some equally vigorous activity. Sounding tones is an especially effective way to release energy through the voice. Obviously, you would want to find some constructive way to release this energy, for it never helps to react destructively, thus adding to the trouble and confusion already disturbing the atmosphere.

Music is another means to discharge strong, angry feelings and energies, while at the same time in the alchemy of exchange, music refills you with its own cleansing currents and healing essences. Release and receive!

Interestingly, I have found that in times of anger different persons react very differently. Some will go to any extremes to avoid controversy and conflict; others just want to be quiet; still others attack and even look for ways to blow off steam in assertive, fiery, combustible outbursts. Because of these varied reactions, I would recommend several different types of music which will help to release your anger through various means of expression.

Strong Music to Air Out Anger

Beethoven - Egmont Overature
Tchaikovsky - Symphony No. 5 (last movement)
Saint Saens - Symphony No. 3 (Organ), last
　　movement
Rheinberger - Organ Concertos
Janáček - Sinfonietta
Wagner - Ride of the Valkyries
　　Prelude to Lohengrin (Act 3)
Poulenc - Concerto for Organ, Timpani and Strings
Ginastera - Estancia
Brahms - Piano Concerto No. 1

The above musical selections are good for receiving and absorbing angry feelings. These pieces are powerful and large enough to contain your release. Another approach, however, is to use music to calm and rebalance strong emotions through more quiet and less outwardly dramatic pieces. Very often they will help you to relax at all levels and release anger through transmutation inside yourself. In the midst of angry feelings, these pieces will either rebalance you, making you wonder how you could have become so agitated with temper, or they will make you move toward positive outer expression of the anger by lifting it into a constructive activity.

Quiet Music to Calm Anger

Bach, J.S. - Two Concertos for Two Pianos
Handel - Harp Concerto
Roth - You Are the Ocean
Halpern-Kelly - Ancient Echoes
Schubert - Prelude to Rosamunde
Dowland - Lute Music
Gluck - Dance of the Blessed Spirits
Dexter - Golden Voyage I
Van Eyck - Music for Recorder
Andy Williams

See the appendix for more suggestions, along with label numbers.

It is important to experience your music privately—in the intimacy of your own home—and at times it is also beneficial to go to live concerts. Music in the home can flow into you with little interference or "static" from other persons and vibrations. On the other hand, a powerful live concert that is a happening gathers a whole audience and lifts it into a higher group consciousness, either through group emotional clearance or even a spiritual experience. Buy live recordings whenever possible.

Certain performing artists serve as charged vehicles for emotional communication among an audience; their artistry is an agent to help others to transmute negative feelings into positive emotional outpouring, through the medium of music. I have experienced this response while listening to a live performance by Artur Rubinstein, and another, by Vladimir Horowitz. Rubinstein's joy and delight with life sparkle through the music that he plays and the people who hear his concerts. His feelings are infectious, and they help to raise many low spirits. Horowitz channels great power, and delivers electricity through his playing. Listeners are stimulated with high voltage energy by his masterful technique, combined with inner power and vitality. From the most quiet, delicate pianissimos to the mightiest crescendos, Horowitz spans the keyboard and the chords of human emotions. The music that he performs releases coils of directed energy that charge the audience with new strength and remove various blockages of repressed feelings and memories. In a recent interview, Horowitz stated that one of his greatest aims in making music is to have the piano sound like an orchestra, and thus his playing is a full spectrum of sound that bathes the listener throughout his whole being—physical, emotional, mental and soul.

Johnny Cash. In a different way, the country singer, Johnny Cash, with his renditions of ballads, gospel songs and personal folk music, elicits sustained emotional catharsis from his audience. Cash is like a folk hero to many of his fans. He has come through many personal challenges and tragedies and emerges before his audience singing and pushing ahead with a courageous spirit of overcoming. I have felt Johnny Cash, in his own unique way, creating strong emotional rapport with those who hear him. He dresses in black. His voice is not smooth, but it contains a rough-hewn honesty and a strong, gutsy quality which empathizes with the human condition and personal suffering. His songs combine strength and compassion, the masculine and feminine poles of feeling, which finally neither condone nor condemn.

Johnny Cash's songs proclaim a yearning for freedom on the open road, the desire in the human heart to overcome confinements and find love and union with another person—a dream that is often thwarted by the "fates" and frailties of earthly existence. Listen to the tremendous out-pouring of feeling which Cash generated when he visited San Quentin and Folsom Prison to do live concerts for the inmates. These powerful recordings are testimony to the basic longings of mankind, no matter how seemingly distorted, for some ineffable union in the Spirit. In their own way they are analagous to the heart-rending synthesis of joy and sorrow which Horowitz achieves in his playing a live performance of Rachmaninoff's Piano Concerto No. 3.

Behind many of Cash's songs, as performed on the guitar, harmonica and the human voice, there is the con-tinuous, driving rhythm of a fiery locomotive, steaming along its tracks, gaining momentum and breaking into freedom and total release. The sound of the powering express train evokes in me the yearning of the human soul to break free of its earthly prisons and confinements, and to roar its joy with smoke and whistle, as it grinds toward open spaces.

In these ways Johnny Cash generates raw energy and a powerful emotional bond in his audience. I definitely feel that his music is stimulating, for it does contain strong waves of feeling which arouse the listener in very grounded, earthy ways. Cash takes us away with him, but he brings us back—now more savvy and compas-sionate—to help and share what he has learned through life's suffering.

Play Johnny Cash's songs when you are feeling strongly about facing challenges in the physical world and when you wish to release your emotions into daily rounds, perhaps venting nostalgic memories.

Relieving Tension. Sometimes the schedules of a busy day might make you tense. You may feel wound up, physically and emotionally, like a tightly coiled wire. To unwind and to slow down, you may need to play music that is more quiet, melodically pleasing and slower in rhythm and pacing. Here are some suggestions for you to use:

Music for Hyperactivity

Bach, J.S. - Air on a G String
McKuen - Concerto for Balloon and Orchestra
Grieg - Holberg Suite
Beethoven - Symphony No. 6 (first and second
    movements)
Pachelbel - Canon in D
Hovhaness - Mysterious Mountain
Mozart - Concerto for Flute and Harp
Vivaldi - Flute Concertos
    Four Seasons
Giuliani - Guitar Concertos
Mantovani

Depression and Fear. If you are feeling dejected, tired and negative about life, then most likely you should go to sleep. Before getting the rest you need, play a quiet piece of music, such as the ones mentioned above. If sleep is not possible, or you are not tired but just low and feeling the "blues," then you need some music that will lift you out of gloom. I suggest these musical selections which can pierce through melancholy, fears, doubts and apprehensions:

Music for Depression and Fear

Delibes - Coppelia
Beethoven - Piano Concerto No. 5 (Emperor)
Dvorak - Symphony No. 8
    Slavonic Dances
Mozart - Symphony No. 35 (Haffner)
Handel - Water Music
    Music for the Royal Fireworks
Grofe - Grand Canyon Suite
Mendelssohn - Symphony No. 4 (Italian)
Parry - Jerusalem

Handel - Choruses from Messiah and Israel in
  Egypt
Rachmaninoff - Piano Concerto No. 2 (final
  movement)

Sometimes boredom is caused by a lack of variety in our schedules, or an unimaginative, ungrateful attitude toward our task. "Rut" implies a need either to change our attitude or our approach to the assignment. Find the best proportion for each day, in which you combine regularity and spontaneity. There will also be certain spaces in your life, called "open key periods," in which you are between "assignments." These are times of great opportunity, if you approach them creatively and with receptivity. Music can be a stimulus to help in these areas.

However, if you use such free times to worry, or waste them in idleness, you will lose a great gift, and you will look back later, seeing how you could have used this time more wisely. There is always so much to learn, so many areas in which you can grow, that it is extremely wasteful to feel bored or limited. These musical selections awaken new enthusiasm, vision and vitality:

Music to Relieve Boredom

Liszt - Hungarian Rhapsodies
Respighi - Ancient Dances and Airs; Pines of Rome
F.J. Haydn - Trumpet Concerto
Rodrigo - Concierto Aranjuez
  Fantasy for a Courtier
Rimsky-Korsakov - Scheherazade
Prokofiev - Lt. Kije
Koto Mozart

Strength and Courage. At the times in your life when you need greater courage—either to make a decision or to stand firm in the path you have chosen—music can help greatly to strengthen your determination and constructive will power.

A friend who has long struggled with a compulsion to overeat went through many programs of self-help, including weight-watching programs, nutrition classes, and the like, but her main problem was lack of self-discipline—simply not being able to use her will power to push herself away from the table. She found that certain musical pieces served as chargings to stand up to her demanding appetite. By listening to specific musical selections, she was able to conquer excess and to eat more intelligently. She used Kabalevsky's "Comedians" and Rozsa's "Ben Hur."

Another friend uses music to help him meet difficulties in business relationships. Just before going out to deal with a difficult person, he plays certain powerful musical pieces that gear him for the challenge. Being by nature rather retiring and peace-loving, he finds that these musical choices galvanize him sufficiently to stand up for his position. He no longer allows himself to be bullied, and the music gives him courage, without making him overly aggressive or tyrannical.

Here are some suggestions for music that will awaken deeper courage in you. This music is also a stimulant to the physical body. It often causes increase of blood flow, speed of circulation and increased muscular energy and metabolism.

Music for Strength and Courage

Elgar - Pomp and Circumstances March, No. 1
Beethoven - Piano Concerto No. 5 (Emperor)
  Choral Fantasy for Piano and Orchestra
Brahms - Symphony No. 2 (final movement)
Battle Hymn of the Republic
La Marseillaise (arranged by Hector Berlioz)
Berlioz - Harold in Italy (third and fourth
  movements)
Copland - A Lincoln Portrait
  Suite of Old American Songs

R. Strauss - Sunrise (from Thus Sprach
  Zarathustra)
Star Spangled Banner

Relaxation and Reverie. After a long day at work, there
will be times when you may wish just to put your feet up
and relax. As some persons prefer to use this time to
mellow with a glass of wine or brood creatively with a
newspaper, you may wish to use music to help you unwind. Certain music allows you to tune in to wistful,
nostalgic memories—enchantments and places of fantasy
that you can visit in consciousness, if not in actual physical
travel.

Music for Relaxation and Reverie

Wagner - Evening Star (from Tannhauser)
Zamfir - Romantic Flute of Pan
Debussy - Clair de lune;
  Sacred and Profane Dances for Harp and
    Orchestra
Ravel - Pavane for a Dead Princess
Halpern-Kelly - Ancient Echoes
Rosewood and Silver
Parkening Plays Bach (Guitar solo)
Stivell - Renaissance of the Celtic Harp
Lee - Celestial Spaces for Koto
Bruch - Scottish Fantasy
Kreisler - Humoresque
Copland - Quiet City;
  Appalachian Spring
Vivaldi - Oboe Concertos

Love and Devotion. Erich Fromm, in his book, *The Art
of Loving*, has written that love is a decision, not an emotion. In the midst of all temporary ups and downs in your
life, you have, innately within you, an enormous God-
given power, the greatest power, which is to express
unconditional *love*. It is really constant love and devotion,
with understanding and discernment, that will fill your
relationships with joys and overcomings.

Certain pieces of music, with their melodies and sonorities, will help to awaken the power of love within you. These pieces appeal directly to your heart center, and they will bathe you in love-energy.

As a general rule such music emphasizes the high strings of the orchestra, the harp and the organ. Some of these pieces have been composed for the whole orchestra, which will "bombard" your atmosphere more powerfully than just a few instruments or chamber music. Such pieces are like great beams of light (to some they often appear as rose and blue) that penetrate you and your environment, thus filling every space with the devotional energies of love.

Music for Love and Devotion

Franck - Panis Angelicus
Denver-Domingo - Perhaps Love
Rachmaninoff - Love Theme
   (18th Variation from Rhapsody on a Theme of
   Paganini)
Grieg - I Love Thee
Wagner - Liebestod (from Tristan und Isolde)
   Prelude to Act 1 (Parsifal)
Herbert - Ah, Sweet Mystery of Life
Marian Anderson - Spirituals
Jessye Norman - Sacred Songs
Pavarotti - O Sole Mio
J.S. Bach - Jesu, Joy of Man's Desiring
Mahalia Jackson - Miscellaneous Hymns
Soundtrack - Somewhere in Time
Mendelssohn - Violin Concerto
Parkening Plays Bach (Guitar Solo)

In a recent television interview, Seiji Ozawa, conductor of the Boston Symphony Orchestra, said the way great music has helped him the most is to make him feel a particular emotion such as happy or sad in hundreds of different ways. The various instrumental colors, melodies and harmonies of music stimulate many overtones and subtleties of feeling. Music helps us to get in touch with that total palette of feeling inside, and it calls us to externalize those feelings in our relationships, in conversation, in worship, or in the expression of common goals worked out together. We can use the profound content of music to awaken the feeling part of ourselves.

Explore the wide range of musical choices that have been suggested. Find those pieces that help you the most to contact, release and refine your total spectrum of emotional response.

CLEAR THINKING, MENTAL POWER

Just as certain selections of music will nourish your physical body and your emotional layer, so other musical works will bring greater health to your mind. Music can help you find greater mental clarity and focus.

Your attitudes affect tremendously what happens to you and what kind of day you meet. As experience, itself, is neutral, it is your attitude, your thoughts and feelings, that determine largely what you will make of your challenges and opportunities. It is the sign of a healthy mind when we see but do not judge, holding no limiting, rigid opinions based on the past, and are alive to thoughts and new possibilities. Such a mind is alert, observant, and a well-directed instrument of the soul. As your mind can remain flexible, expectant and clearly attuned, so will your life bring you many new opportunities.

Generally, music most pleasing to the mind will be clear melodically and rhythmically. Often, the strings will appeal to the mind and give it focus. Music of the baroque period is ordered, melodic and contains few surprises. It tends to flow along pleasingly, like vibrant currents of a river. Such music helps the mind to focus, plan and execute the thoughts and desires you are seeking to fulfill.

Much music of the twentieth century is also intellectual and well thought out. However, little music of our time is melodic, so although the structure is well thought out, it tends to grate on the listener (at least this listener) and is often hard logic without deep feeling or inspiration. Cultivate music that inspires you; avoid computerized, mental sounds, composed out of mere curiosity or cleverness. Certain selections will help you move into your day with planning and directed energy. Here are some musical pieces for a more healthy, attuned mind:

Music for Clear Thinking

J.S. Bach - Brandenburg Concertos
   The Well-Tempered Clavier
Soundtrack - Born Free
Tibetan Bells
Psalms of David (sung by Kings College Choir)
Telemann - Concerto for Three Violins and
   Orchestra
Weber - Oberon Overture
Brahms - Violin Concerto
Scarlatti - Harpsichord Sonatas
Handel - Water Music
Orchestral music of J.S. Bach
Baroque string music of Telemann, Vivaldi,
   Albinoni, Corelli, Torelli, and others.

MUSIC AND MEDITATION

The greatest, most inspiring music speaks to your soul. Such wonderful, timeless melodies and harmonies link you with the Eternal. As you can let yourself move inside these masterpieces, you will feel Light-filled, attuned and in communion with the Creator of Life. Such music will always send you back into the world with renewed hope, vigor and joyful serenity. You may feel that you are accompanied by innumerable hosts of God who call you to let go of all negativity and heaviness so that you can receive higher frequencies of energy. Such music brings God's worlds near.

Your deepest experience of music becomes a spiritual sacrament. No longer are you interested only in bettering earthly conditions. You are now entering Light. Go into the Eternal Presence, opening yourself to God's unlimited guidance. There will be many times of meditation and prayer when you will want to keep totally silent. However, a very special piece of music can prepare you for your devotions. Such music will still your body, emotions and mind, so that your soul center can speak through you, grounding whatever Light is available.

Here are some guidelines to prepare for a more effective meditation preceded by music:

1. Begin by treating this musical meditation as a holy time. Listen in an attitude of reverence and praise. You may want to speak an affirmation or Bible verse. For example:

"I will pray with the Spirit and with understanding also." (I Corinthians 14:15)

"The music of the heavens fills me with God's Light."

2. Be open to the spiritualizing energies of the music. Something will happen to you spiritually as you are listening.

3. Keep a notebook handy, by your chair, so that you can jot down any impressions you receive.

4. Notice any impressions that the melodies might awaken in you. (These may come in the form of places, colors, presences, shapes, archetypes, ideas, and so forth.)

5. Ask yourself, "What feelings does the music awaken in me?" (These may be joy, peace, power, warmth, or some other feeling.)

6. In what part of your body do you feel the music the most? (For example, in the groin, stomach, solar plexus, heart, throat, forehead, crown of head, muscles, joints.) It is important to realize consciously *where* you feel the music. This is a signal that either more energy is needed in this area, or that diffusing the energy is what is called for.

In this sense, the music serves as a balancing device and will help to harmonize your system.

7. When the music has finished, lift up your heart in thankfulness for the good that the music has brought you.

Gradually, you will find those special pieces of music that best lead you into the silence. Keep a list of the selections that attune you the best. Play them often and know that you can depend upon them to help you deepen your sensitivity to the Divine Presence.

These are some of the musical selections I have found to be most helpful in times of meditation, prayer, and heightened devotion:

Music for Meditation and Prayer

Vaughan Williams - Fantasia on a Theme of
    Thomas Tallis
Palestrina - Pope Marcellus Mass
Paul Horn - Inside the Taj Mahal
Humperdinck - Children's Prayer (from Hansel and
    Gretel)
Handel - Largo (from Xerxes)
Dvořák - Largo (from Symphony No. 9)
Elgar - Nimrod (from Enigma Variations)
J.S. Bach - Come Sweet Death
    Toccata and Fugue (orchestral version)
Bruckner - Symphony No. 8 (third movement)
Wagner - Prelude to Act 1 (from Lohengrin)
Fauré - In Paradise (from Requiem)
McKuen - Concerto for Balloon and Orchestra
John Michael Talbot - Come to the Quiet
Flowers from the Silence
Mozart - Vesperae Solennes de Confessore
    (Sanctus)
    Ave Verum Corpus

The appendix contains more suggestions for all these categories, along with label numbers.

From the many different suggestions in this chapter, you will discover those musical selections that are most appealing to you. It is quite likely that some of your tastes will change, according to events, cycles and processes in your life. But you will find those pieces of music that will remain with you all your days, like faithful friends. Keep these favorites near you; sing their melodies and let them sound through you. Also, develop new friends and favorites among your musical acquaintances.

3

Finding Your Music

> My purpose is to create music for all people,
> music which is beautiful and healing, to at-
> tempt what old Chinese painters called "spirit
> resonance" in melody and sound.
>
> Alan Hovhaness

Many factors influence our musical needs and choices.
Among these are the following: 1) temperament; 2) sensory responses; 3) behavioral patterns and childhood
memories; 4) home and work environment; and 5) strong
desires and aspirations, the ideals we follow most in this
lifetime.

Each of us was born with a specific temperament to
master and express throughout our lifetime. Each person's
temperament is unique and will never again be repeated.
The Creator's Light and our own vital responses come
through our temperaments in varied shadings of energy,
called the four elements: Fire, Earth, Air and Water.
Spiritual teachings through the ages have recognized these
four modes for life's expression. The ancient Greeks considered the four elements to be definite psychological
forces, which correspond in the person to the will (Fire),
the body and action (Earth), the mind and thinking (Air),
and the emotions (Water). These life forces are powers,

potentially present in each of us, in different combinations and proportions. In astrological teachings, Fire refers to the sun signs—Aries, Leo and Sagittarius; Earth refers to the energies of Taurus, Virgo and Capricorn; Air describes the energies of Gemini, Libra and Aquarius; and Water suggests the energies of Cancer, Scorpio and Pisces. Each of us expresses God's Light and our own life desires and purposes through the particular blending of these four elements in our temperaments. We cannot change our temperaments, but we can express more constructively through them. For observation and insight, we might discover that one or two elements are dominant while one element might be extremely recessive and dormant, thus requiring extra attention and focus, so that we can release more Light through it when necessary.

Find yourself in the four elements as they are described below. Such understanding can help you begin to release more of your inherent talents and potentialities through these channels for Light, to develop your strengths and work on your weaknesses and blind spots. *Use music*, too, to cultivate and activate your expression of energies, as they emerge through the four temperaments.

FIRE

This area of the temperament is very intense and "high-voltage." It acts instantly and gives off sparks. On the negative side, it can be too impulsive, speaking out or moving before thinking. The fiery element can be tense, hyperactive, domineering and judgmental, at times taking issue or criticizing before considering others' intentions. The fiery side likes to win, eagerly accepting challenge and competition. Usually, it is fearless, and sometimes fool-hardy. At other times, the fiery side considers itself too highly and becomes inflated with pride and ego. When being expressed negatively, the fire side often goes off on a power trip, willing to do anything to be the star of the show. Its flames then cause constant turmoil.

When the fiery side acts constructively, the person can be a dynamic leader, a confronting, courageous pioneer, and a fearless worker who can make necessary decisions quickly and move forward. Positive fire energy is decisive, yet teachable, explosive but not destructive, fast, yet patient with those who are slower or of differing opinions. Even with its strong direction, constructive fire energy expresses appreciation and consideration for others. It emanates self-worth without seeming superior and pompous.

KEYNOTE: In developing the Fire in us, we need to love and purify, avoid impulsiveness, aggressiveness and insensitivity.

Musically, our fiery nature likes *power*, surging sound, strong rhythms, and romantic, yet dynamic melodies, music of strength. I have observed that the fiery element often responds well to music of victory:

Music of Fire

J.S. Bach - Toccata and Fugue (orchestral version, cond. Stokowski)
Wagner - Overture and Prelude to Die Meistersinger
　　Ride of the Valkyries
　　Dawn and Siegfried's Rhine Journey
　　(from Die Gotterdammerung)
Beethoven - Choral Fantasy for Piano and Chorus and Orchestra
　　Symphony No. 9
　　Symphony No. 5
Verdi - Grand March (from Aida)
Rachmaninoff - Piano Concertos Nos. 2 and 3
D'Indy - Symphony on a French Mountain Air
Sibelius - Finlandia
Suppé - Poet and Peasant Overture
　　Light Cavalry Overture

F.J. Haydn - The Creation
  The Seasons
  Masses
Fanshawe - African Sanctus
  Misa Luba
  Misa Criolla

EARTH

The Earth side of the temperament tends to be cautious, concrete and old-fashioned. It emphasizes details, practicality, mundane activities, set routine and stability. It needs security to be at ease. This side of our temperament is dependable, gradual, and follows orders well, and stresses usefulness. Rarely does it welcome changes, daring imagination, new opinions, ideas or ventures into the unknown. It is modest, loyal, and moves to keep things clear. It keeps closely to plans and budgets; it measures.

When the Earth side acts constructively, it is constant without being rigid, and it is restful without being lethargic. Likewise, it is definite and traditional without being judgmental or provincial. The Earth side deeply feels and appreciates the beauty of the good earth and of nature. It thrives on activity that beautifies the home and earthly places, such as gardening and interior decorating. It is happy doing manual work and achieving practical results.

KEYNOTE: In developing Earth we will be steadfast and practical but must avoid rigidity, inertia, and provincial, judgmental attitudes by expanding horizons and interests.

Musically, the Earth side seeks melodies that are warm, homey, traditional, and evocative of friendship and earthly comforts. Music of nature appeals to it, especially that which is nostalgic and suggestive of repose. Since this side likes practicality, it often favors music with definite lyrics and meaningful poetry. It prefers literal statement to mere suggestiveness. Simple themes, often repeated, appeal to it, especially beautiful, restful tunes.

The warm, poignant melodies of Stephen Foster celebrate the home and domestic happiness, both of which delight the Earth side. Other pieces that will be in tune with Earth include the following selections, which are warm, melodically pleasing and definite in form.

Music of Earth

Dvořák - Cello Concerto
  Overture to Nature, Life and Love
  Silent Woods
  Humoresque
Brahms - Lullaby
  Symphony No. 3
Bruch - Scottish Fantasy
  Violin Concerto No. 1
Massenet - Meditation (from Thais)
Debussy - Clair de lune
Fauré - Requiem
Goldmark - Rustic Wedding Symphony
Music of Irving Berlin
Songs of Perry Como, Bing Crosby, Barbara
  Mandrell, John Denver, Gordon Bok, Johnny
  Mathis, Captain and Tennille, Johnny Cash,
  Barry Manilow, etc.
Music of Puccini

AIR

The Air element in our temperament is mercurial; like a chameleon, it is constantly changing, according to the present company, thoughts, and the impressions absorbed from the environment. Air begins with the more mental and conceptual, moving from the abstract into the concrete and practical situations. It enjoys the perpetual motion of ideas and theories, and it seeks endless variety. It is rarely contemplative but often avoids hard, physical work. The Air side likes to fantasize, and then disowns its dreams when they become too demanding. It is very independent and resents restrictions. The airy part of the nature thinks before it feels and tends to analyze every situation and person. Sometimes it sees only its own point of view and is insensitive to others' feelings or perspectives. It can be shallow and selfish.

At its best, the Air side considers with clarity and thinks through difficulties to find the best solution. It probes and penetrates, making sudden connections and penetrating obstacles with energies that cleanse and direct. Most constructively, the Air side synthesizes, seeing the best in every person and challenge and combining forces to promote greater well-being and creativity. It is versatile and varied, like the many facets of a diamond, and can draw upon talents and powers to meet every need. Usually it is objective and wastes little time showing sentiment.

To develop the Air in us we need to explore ideas and possibilities. We need to learn to follow through and avoid scatteredness and superficiality. It is important to communicate clearly with focus.

Musically, the Air side needs rhythmical variety and clear melodies. It likes music that moves ahead in a certain direction, yet encompasses a wide spectrum of style and color. It responds to experimental music, such as the twelve-tone scale and various aleatoric works. Extroverted music appeals to Air, especially current songs and promotional hit tunes, though too much emotion in music is puzzling. Contemporary sounds and textures fascinate it for a short period until it becomes bored.

Here are some musical selections with strong rhythms and movement and many colors that the Air side might find enjoyable.

Music of Air

Iasos - Angels of Comfort
Shankar - Indian Ragas
  Concerto for Sitar

Holdridge - Other Side of the Mountain, Part 2
    Music of Holdridge
Born Free (Soundtrack)
Mozart - Horn Concertos
    Clarinet Concerto
Gershwin - Rhapsody in Blue
    Piano Concerto in F
Rodgers - Slaughter on Tenth Avenue
Tibetan Bells
Elgar - Enigma Variations
Joplin - Rags
Poulenc - Rustic Concerto for Harpsichord and
    Orchestra
Songs of Bob Dylan, Mason Williams, Judy Col-
    lins, Gordon Lightfoot and Dan Fogelburg
R. Strauss - Don Juan
    A Hero's Life

WATER

The fourth aspect of the temperament is expressed through the element of Water. This part is more introspective, emotional, at times brooding and melancholic, even to the point of self-indulgence. It often needs to be alone but not for too long lest it become morbid. We must guard against the watery side's emphasizing the negative and exaggerating a situation or condition. We must avoid its self-pity, self-deprecation, and martyrdom. Still it needs to come forward, out of hiding.

When it can get out of itself—usually by talking out or by feeling others' needs to be more important than its own—this side is very caring, generous and compassionate. At its best, the watery side is loyal beyond its emotional ups and downs. Often, it can feel with a great intuitive perspective, sensing and "knowing" in ways that are not logically explainable.

The watery element grows through experiences of great joy and suffering. When working at its best, the watery side will lift up all tragedy into the Light, overcoming moodiness, pessimism and self-pity. It will find itself best by losing itself in loving service with others and one-pointed devotion to God. Often, its energies will be expressed through dedication to a cause.

KEYNOTE: We could well advise our watery side: "Get out of yourself; forgive and forget; give yourself to something larger than yourself; avoid depleting moods, and fight out of heaviness no matter what the cost. Be joyful!"

Musically, the watery element seeks pieces with deep feeling and contrasting polarities of emotion which bring out a total response from the heart. This side feels before it thinks. If you tend toward the dramatic, musical evocations of melancholy and tragedy will appeal to you. Even more, you enjoy hearing the melodies and power of triumph and victory, as they drive away tears and suffering. Great love themes, deep passions and human striving arouse the watery side with their many moods.

Here are several melodic and dramatic musical selections that will stimulate your Water side:

Music of Water

Handel - Water Music
Pavarotti - Verismo Arias
    My Own Story
    Bravo Pavarotti
Chopin - Nocturnes
DeFalla - Nights in the Gardens of Spain
Koto Flute
J. Strauss - Blue Danube
Tchaikovsky - None But the Lonely Heart
    Symphony No. 6 (Pathetique)
    Romeo and Juliet Overture
Mahler - Symphonies Nos. 4 and 6
Wagner - Prelude and Love-Death (from Tristan
    und Isolde)
Rimsky-Korsakov - Scheherazade

Stivell - Renaissance of the Celtic Harp
Addinsell - Warsaw Concerto
Lara's Theme (from Dr. Zhivago)
Love Theme (from Exodus)
Music of Mantovani
Nat King Cole - Stardust
   When the World was Young
Danny Boy
Bach, J.S. - Come Sweet Death
Bath - Cornish Rhapsody
Rezniček - Donna Diana Overture
Bloch - Schelomo
Joan Baez

YOUR TEMPERAMENT

We cannot change our basic temperament but we can expand it. Relationships of various kinds can help. Seek relationships that call forth your best, but also cultivate friendships and contacts that open new channels for life's expression. Take every opportunity to fill in your blind spots.

Through music you can learn to utilize each element and shading of your temperament more dynamically and beautifully. From the lists you have just read, and other suggestions in the Appendix, you can explore the music that will enhance what you already are or which awakens unexpressed areas in you. If, for example, you find that you may be overemphasizing Fire and Air elements through music that is always loud, heavy, and "fast," bring out new elements in your life by listening to music that is more quiet, reflective and lyrical. You will find that such music will affect your temperament, bringing your life into better balance and tone, and enabling you to approach your relationships as a more well-rounded person who can be more adaptable in every situation.

Share your music with friends, but care about them enough to please them with music that best fits their temperament and needs as well. Use music as a tonic for your life. Enlarge your musical horizons continuously, so that your capacity to express Light grows.

As you choose your music wisely and appropriately, all of your sensory organs will be quickened, and in some cases your whole being will be rebalanced and harmonized.

Visualizing. The visual sense responds to colors, shadings, designs and formations. Great music stimulates the imagination and helps you to picture scenes, persons, places and dimensions of life that become more real to you. The memorable conductor, Charles Munch, mentions this aspect of music when writing these words in his autobiography, *I Am a Conductor* (pp. 9, 54):

> Music is an art that expresses the inexpressible. It rises far above what words can mean or the intelligence define. Its domain is the imponderable and the impalpable land of the unconscious.... Music always suggests something to me: just a color or a landscape or perhaps a sensation that can be felt and expressed only in sound.

The musical compositions of Claude Debussy often awaken in the listener scenes and pictures of water, kingdoms of the sea, the streams in forests. Sounds of a Hawaiian love song conjure up scenes of the islands and beckoning sunsets. A Nat King Cole lyric will recall nostalgic memories and relationships from the past. "Ebb Tide," with its actual sounds of gulls and ocean waves, will remind listeners of beaches, surf, the seashore and endless horizons of life. In another way, Wagner's Prelude to *Lohengrin* (Act I) evokes the archetypal pattern-shape of a chalice, which expresses the theme of the Holy Grail and mankind's quest for spiritual Light and the perfection of his nature in God.

Much well-known program music contains definite stories and themes, which the composer describes through melodies and tone colors. Such music will enhance your visual sensitivity, and it will stimulate your powers of visualization. Unlike television, music will not "do it for you," but instead will cause you to activate your own imagination. No two persons will "see" or feel the music in the same way, and there is no single way or one meaning to look for.

Play musical offerings in a relaxed and expectant attitude. Let the melodies and colors of the music stream through you, evoking whatever scenes or impressions may come. Be open to the music, accepting whatever it might stir up in you. The real wonder and magic of music become clear as you let it "stir up the gift of God within you" (2 Timothy 1:6). You may be taken to other places and dimensions of consciousness, or you may see loved ones and familiar landscapes rising out of deep memories. You may see yourself in new roles, with a different appearance, and you may travel in consciousness to other lands and times. As a visual stimulant, music can help you greatly. Experience a beautiful musical work with full expectancy and let it take you where it will.

Here are a few choice selections of evocative, pictorial music:

Music that Paints Pictures

Beethoven - Symphony No. 6 (Pastorale)
Grieg - Morning (from Peer Gynt)
Debussy - The Sea
  Nocturnes
  The Engulfed Cathedral
Mendelssohn - Symphony No. 3 (Scotch)
Holst - The Planets
Stravinsky - The Firebird
Mussorgsky - Pictures at an Exhibition
Wagner - Evening Star (from Tannhauser)
Berlioz - Fantastic Symphony
Vaughan Williams - Lark Ascending
   Antarctic Symphony
J. Strauss - Blue Danube Waltz

Tchaikovsky - Romeo and Juliet Overture
Respighi - Pines of Rome
  Roman Festivals
Schumann - Symphony No. 1 (Spring)
Ebb Tide

Entering into the sound of music. You will never lose your identity. Rather, you go into the continuum of melodies to link with the timeless, moving eternities of life itself. Music is a world of its own, created by the movement and interaction of energies. Unlike words or physical objects, music is always becoming, always noticeably moving beyond itself. The ephemeral quality of music is beautifully expressed by Anais Nin:

> Music holds the movements of life, the chained incidents which compose it, the eternal melting of one note before another to create song. The notes must melt before one another; they must be lost after they have given their soul, for the sake of the whole. It may be a beautiful note, but it cannot strike alone forever. It must pass, as all things must pass, to make up the immense composition that is life.

Musical sounds, especially melodious ones, lift you out of heaviness and limitations. They help you to break through rigidity and dull repetition. Listen to the expansive tones of a flute and you will begin to fly with wings or flow like wind. Enter the lilt and glissando of harps and you will feel free and weightless, able to rise into lighter atmospheres and expanded feelings. The sound of a cello is deeper and very soulful and it often awakens the feelings of devotion and longing.

Listen, also, to the sounds of nature, flowing streams, the wind playing through trees, bird songs or the surging waves of the ocean. Such living music will help to attune you to celestial, cosmic forces that will inspire and help you. Beautiful music is like a magic carpet, that lifts you into God's grandeur and connects you with the sounding harmonies of the spheres.

Here are a few selected pieces of music that will expand your auditory faculties, always lifting your consciousness:

Music to Expand Hearing

Paul Horn - Inside the Taj Mahal
Carlos (Wendy) - Sonic Seasonings (especially "Fall")
Environments
Dexter - Golden Voyage I, III
Tibetan Bells
Palestrina - Pope Marcellus Mass
Humperdinck - Children's Prayer (from Hansel and Gretel)
Hovhaness - Mysterious Mountain

A certain musical selection may cause you to feel more happy, courageous and loving, while another piece may arouse in you feelings of agitation, anger or confusion. Find music that helps you. Avoid sounds that deplete you and scatter you. Be selective with your music. Fill your life with beautiful sounds, not just background noise. Cultivate upliftment from your music.

Notice where your music affects you. Does it expand your heart center, making you feel more loving and filled with good will? Does it stimulate your mind and allow your brain to function with greater clarity? What effects does your music produce in your physical body? Do you feel stronger, more fluid and graceful? Do you feel like dancing in movements that are freeing, or does your music cause you to twitch irritably and shake with agitation and nervous headaches? By becoming aware of areas affected by music, you can use music to direct energy to places that need it or to disperse energy where it is congested.

Cultivate the music that raises and ennobles you, helping you to feel good and energized to accomplish constructive, creative goals. Avoid whatever sounds lower you and deplete you, or reduce you to an uncontrollable, confused, "zombie-like" automaton, easily dominated by negative, destructive forces.

The power of great music can also help you discover and change certain habits and behavior patterns that you kept from childhood. From childhood influences and from even deeper soul memories, we have all absorbed experiences and impressions that remain in us today, like deep finger-prints in the conscious and subconscious mind. Dr. Alexander Lowen (author of *Bioenergetics*) and Moshe Feldenkrais (movement therapist and author of *Awareness through Movement*) are pioneers in showing how the body stores memories in muscles and joints. They have demonstrated in their studies of body response, that even our muscles and whole physical organisms often retain the memories and reflex patterns of the past. Sometimes just one unpleasant childhood memory sticks in us like glue, either locking up our joints and muscles, or cramping our emotions and thought patterns. Exercises of the body can release memories in the mind. Music can facilitate this process and help to release many of the blocks and crisscrosses in the system, even those we may never have consciously realized. Great music can cause increased flow of energy to circulate through the physical body, the emotions, and the mind.

From my classes in music therapy, conducted privately and in schools and nursing homes, I have seen the healing power of music unlock frozen joints and stiff muscles. I have seen a woman begin to move freely in her wheelchair to the sounds of Bizet's *Carmen* ("Toreador's Dance"); later she smiled and released even more fear and tension as she listened to Chopin's waltzes. Another patient—a man who was so often quarrelsome and difficult to manage—became more helpful after hearing Bach's *Brandenburg Concertos* and a Haydn symphony.

The great composer Sergei Rachmaninoff found deep healing through his own Piano Concerto No. 2. His main challenge was to overcome depression, largely caused by childhood scenes and the feelings of separation and homesickness he felt for his native Russia. He made headway in this challenge through the practice of visualization, mental suggestion, and through the vibrations of music.

You too, can find those musical pieces that will pierce through a mood, a repressed memory, or a blocked area in yourself. Here are some directives to help your progress:

Recall and release the past. Choose three of your favorite pieces of music that you love deeply because they make you feel good. Begin to listen to these pieces, keeping a notebook next to you. Be aware of how and where you are feeling the music. Then, allow yourself to go back into your childhood; be open to scenes and memories stored deep inside you. Allow these to surface and write them down.

In an attitude of gratefulness and acceptance, ask the Eternal Presence to reveal to you, through music, what it is that you need to know in order to remove the block or hindrance you might be feeling. It may be an early scene with parents or brothers and sisters. It may be the memory of a pet, a painful sight or sound, a personal disappointment. Or there may be something in your life that is still unfinished—something you feel you must complete.

Closure, or dealing with unfinished business, at least to some extent, is often necessary before we can go forward. If death or separation makes this closure physically impossible, you can still talk, feel, and act out constructively *now*, to release whatever you have held inside for so long. If necessary, imagine the person you wish to speak to; see the person sitting in an empty chair; speak to that individual as you would want to if he/she were sitting in front of you. As you speak out loud, in the present tense, let the music drain out of you whatever deep feelings you wish to release. Feel yourself letting go of long-held emotions that have cramped and stifled you. Complete *now*, in a loving and constructive way, whatever has frustrated you and remained incomplete inside you. Avoid deliberately hurtful and destructive responses, for these will only prolong discord and will deplete your energies. At the same time, do not be insincere nor overly polite. Through music, you can speak firmly, honestly and lovingly to another; you can allow yourself to forgive and be forgiven; and you can find the best ways to complete unfinished, unresolved, unexpressed experiences, which have been weighing on you for too long. Guilt feelings from the past can be released creatively *now*.

Great music can bring many kinds of solutions. It can help you to repair broken relationships and inspire you to build new ones. Beautiful music also stimulates you to overcome your own inertia, negativity and procrastination. The dynamic chargings of great music will not allow you to remain in attitudes of anger, self-pity, frustration, regret or sadness (which is often anger turned inward). Rather, the most healing music will always call you forward and upward, helping you to find ways to release the past and awakening in you joy and creativity. It opens your heart center to feel the energy of unconditional love.

Remember beautiful musical experiences. Keep a journal and scrapbook of favorite musical memories, any favorite experiences in connection with music. Recall a song you learned as a child and try to sing it now; remember your first contact with a musical instrument, either bought or homemade. What concerts do you remember, and what feelings can you recall from experiencing them? Do you have memories of singing in a choir? Did music ever bring you together with new friends? What favorite trips or places do you associate with certain musical pieces? When did you buy your first recording, and what were your feelings as you listened to it playing? Write down in your notebook the treasured memories that great music has brought into your life.

How has music expanded your sensitivity and perspective? How has music enabled you to appreciate more the colors, sound, customs and essences of other nationalities, cultures, religious traditions, and historical periods? How are you using music now to grow, interpersonally and spiritually?

Recently, I sat down and spent an hour recalling the many ways in which music has enriched my life. Partly as a means of sharing with my readers and partly to suggest a possible approach to keeping a musical notebook, I include some of my most intimate memories which music has provided.

Born in New York City, on Broadway, I experienced music early and in great ethnic variety. Even now as I write, I can hear the beautiful Welsh songs and hymns my mother sang throughout the household. Later, as I played on the sidewalks of our neighborhood, I can recall the mixture of international sounds, pouring together from apartment windows, alleys, and storefronts. From Blumental's Laundry up the block, and from Miller's living room on the first floor, I remember soulful Hebrew, cantorial chanting. From across the street came strong, colorful Latin rhythms, rhumbas and festive party music that lasted into the early morning hours. From our courtyard came sounds of a Chinese koto and flute. Behind our apartment building was a small convent with a garden where I heard the songs of birds accompanying the nuns' singing of Gregorian chants and other devotional music, offered up each morning. Getting off our elevator on the eleventh floor, I often heard nostalgic violin melodies, composed by Fritz Kreisler, or lively polkas and Strauss waltzes.

Down on the seventh floor in the apartment of my Russian friend, Nicholas, I first heard the Russian melodies of Tchaikovsky, Glinka, the basso voice of Chaliapin, and the sounds of balalaikas in the night. On Thursday nights I always listened to the Lone Ranger subduing bank robbers with a straight one-two punch, as the outlaw often hit the ground with a thud on the final note of the crescendo from Wagner's "Flying Dutchman Overture." Then, to the thrilling finale of Rossini's "William Tell Overture," the masked man and Tonto rode off into the hills and sunset. Away from home and neighborhood, I sang the devotional hymns and liturgical music of the Episcopalian and Lutheran churches, which we learned in chapel each morning. My first real introduction to opera came when my mother took me to hear Mario Lanza playing the role of Caruso.

My greatest thrill still remains the first time I heard the magic of a symphony orchestra, with more than one hundred musicians making music together. This experience came in the early fifties in Lewisohn Stadium in New York City when a young, crew-cut Japanese visitor to America named Seiji Ozawa led the orchestra at sunset in a dynamic performance of Tchaikovsky's Fourth Symphony. I have always felt close to Ozawa and have even dreamed of talking with him. Perhaps this is because of these clear memories of his arrival in America, or because I happened to be working near Boston when he began his tenure as Music Director and Conductor of the magnificent Boston Symphony Orchestra. Most recently, I have admired the good work Ozawa and his associates are carrying on through their friendship with China and their mutual sharing and playing of great music, East and West. I deeply enjoyed seeing Ozawa leading an orchestra from his native land, as they experienced common aspirations of brotherhood while playing Beethoven's Ninth Symphony.

I remember, also, the feeling of joy and grandeur, of being swept up into power one morning in Riverside Church after a sermon by the guest speaker, Dr. Martin Luther King. More than 3000 people rose and sang together the "Battle Hymn of the Republic," and the organist, Virgil Fox, played the mighty pipe organ with such full potency that I could feel deep vibration and expansion through my heart center and solar plexus. That morning, the giant sanctuary was filled with cascades of melody. A deep religious fervor in the large congregation reached upward and seemed to join with the singing of heavenly choirs, descending to inspire us. It seemed that those present were lifted out of themselves for a few minutes to spiral upward, above Grant's Tomb, across the street, and then even higher than the huge cathedral tower, reaching to the sky.

Since the day of my twelfth birthday when I bought my first records in an old bookstore near the Bronx Zoo—two musty 78's containing Mozart's 40th Symphony and Beethoven's "Egmont Overture"—music has been with me like a holy companion. Although I am not yet a performing artist, I have found music to be an intimate friend that has continuously enriched my life.

Likewise, music has often been a gateway into God's Presence and the kingdoms that serve him. At various times, the magnetic currents of great music have made me feel both humble and invincible. Through music I have experienced a joy beyond words and genuine glimpses into Light which can only be called mystical and profoundly spiritual.

I recall the statement of the composer, Berlioz, that music and love are "the two wings of the soul," and I agree with these inspired words from the great composer, Frederick Delius:

> Music is a cry of the soul. It is a revelation, a thing to be reverenced. Performances of a great musical work are for us what the rites and festivals of religion were to the ancients—an initiation into the mysteries of the human soul.

Music can change our moods, energize us, lift us to spiritual heights. Everyday sounds affect us, too. Consider for a few minutes to what degree sounds influence your life. What kinds of sounds surround your home and working environments the most? How many of these sounds are pleasing to you? Which give you energy upliftment, and which sounds that you hear each day are confusing, noisy, chaotic or depleting? The psychiatrist James E. Johnson in his book *Freedom From Depression* advocates wholesome music but cautions against the adverse effects of contemporary beats and cacaphony of rock-and-roll which he feels is masquerading as music. He has found beats in this kind of music contribute dangerously to depression and hypertension. This observation has been surfacing repeatedly from many disciplines, but a decrease in the popularity of rock is unlikely since it gathers billions of profit dollars.

Dr. John Diamond, in his excellent and informative book *Your Body Doesn't Lie*, talks about how sound and music play a very large role in our lives. Dr. Diamond is a well-known therapist in the field of behavioral kinesiology, or the study of bodily movement and response based upon energies within the system and in the environment. He writes the following (p. 98):

> Surrounded by the right sounds, we all can be invigorated, energized, and balanced. It has been demonstrated clincially that music adds to our general health and well-being. Music, then, can be an important part of our program of primary prevention—the prevention of illness at the prephysical, energy-imbalance level.

Given the importance of music in our lives, the next question is "Which music is the best?" In the later pages of his book, Dr. Diamond shares the findings of careful research—findings which correlate with other researchers'—into the effects of music on plants and the human organism. He measured muscle response after listening to music, and he reports (p. 100):

> Using hundreds of subjects, I found that listening to rock music frequently causes all the muscles in the body to go weak. The normal pressure required to overpower a strong deltoid muscle in an adult male is about 40 to 45 pounds. When rock music is played, only 10 to 15 pounds is needed.

> ...every major muscle of the body relates to an organ. This means that all the organs of our body are being affected by a large proportion of the popular music to which we are exposed each day. If we add up the hours of radio play throughout the world, we can see how enormous a problem this is.

After careful research, I can agree with these findings. Dr. Diamond discovered that some rock music, such as that of the Beatles, does not have this effect, but the rhythm itself tends to be harmful. He says (p. 105):

> The abnormal rhythm of the rock beat (anapestic - da-da-DA) and the volume of noise level [combine] to induce weakness in us. Noise may be defined as sound which, when it reaches a certain level of intensity, decreases body energy. Detrimental music reduces energy at any volume. Good music and nearly all natural sounds strengthen at any level. But even if you play good music so loudly over a sound system that distortion occurs, a level will be reached at which the sound weakens.

Studies have shown that certain music, if listened to repeatedly, has the effect of depleting one's energy systems and causes confusion in thinking, disorientation of feeling and a reversal of value systems. It has been reported that listening to too many discordant sounds produces a numbness in the body and a confusion between the two sides of the brain, which seems to cause responses and perceptions to switch from one side of the brain to the other less appropriate side. This seems to impair the person's sensitivity so that ugliness becomes an addiction. Such people begin to seek chaos consciously, disturbances and disorder in life because they have lost the perception to judge or distinguish what is beneficial from what is harmful and destructive. In effect when they have reached this point, they have lost all sensitivity to beauty and positive values and will crave totally that which is destroying them. Confusion grows and the lack of resistance eventually can lead to complete zombieism until they have no control over themselves or their actions. A modern author, Albert Roustit, in his book *Prophecy in Music* describes this condition (p. 217):

> The distinction between and music and noise seems to be blurring: melody and words are being replaced by shrieks for which the only accompaniment is a frenetic rhythm, and the result, as we have all, many times observed, is a sort of collective hysteria similar to that of primitive people.
>
> To put oneself into a trance under the effect of rhythmic excitation is to momentarily leave the civilized state to fall into a savage one, at which point, from the depths of human nature, the individual's bestiality makes its appearance too strongly for a weakened spirituality to correct.

Unfortunately, this state has become the norm today so that persons usually under the influence of hard rock need their own "detoxification" process, or some new exposure in healthy conditions to realize that there is an alternative to noise (either silence or beautiful, harmonious sound). Usually, such an alternative becomes possible only in a time of sickness or when choice is no longer an option. This is why future "healing environments" will be controlled, especially in the area of the music that is played inside them. (See Ismael, *The Healing Environment*.)

Even the anticipation of certain music can dehumanize unsuspecting listeners. We all carry our primitive ancestors with us. Some sounds can lower us to what we were in consciousness a long time ago, while other melodies and music will carry us forward, ennobling and lifting our entire being toward greater refinement, beauty, creativity, and evolution out of degeneracy, cruelty and even criminal activity. To a large degree, "You are what you hear."

Today we stand at a crossroads. More than ever, mankind is resisting man-UNkind, both within himself and in the outer environment. Light and destructive forces are becoming increasingly polarized. To move ahead into a new awakening, we are faced with many important decisions and choices, even in the music we buy and listen to. One group of young people recently gathered all their recordings of destructive, chaotic music and burned them in public. The burning pyre of records was a statement against what they considered to be ugly, degrading musical influences in their lives. They decided to go in a different direction while they still had the sensitivity to choose.

Destructive music causes damage, not only to your physical body, but to your emotions and mental processes. Such sounds affect your entire aura, making you feel psychically torn apart, fragmented, frightened, combative, isolated, tense and aimless. Such stressful, ugly sounds will also scatter your plans, and they will fog and frustrate your goals. Most tragically, discordant music will alienate you from your inner center of guidance, cutting you off from your conscious union with the Creator, leaving you feeling abandoned, and exposing you to being controlled by negative vibrations. And, as Dorothy Retallack and others have proved, ugly rock music will kill plants.

How much more joyous and effective life can become as we bring beautiful melodies into our daily environment. The outstanding Finnish composer, Jean Sibelius, was right when he said that *melody* is the soul of great, healing music. In following chapters and in the Appendix you can discover more of those musical selections that will nourish you with their renewing melodies, rhythms and harmonies. Others will hear the music you are playing, and if they are receptive to such music, it will grow on them, until they will actually come to expect it.

What are your deepest aspirations this lifetime? Are they centered mainly in worldly achievement? Are they mostly in the areas of social acceptance and peer relationship? Are they focused mainly in the home and family intimacy, or artistic expression, or scientific pursuit? Or are they largely invisible, inward desires to know and love the Creator more through increased service? Whatever the desire, you can use music to help these dreams come true. Suggestions in this book can help you to find those musical selections that speak to you most deeply and empower you toward your greatest desires and life purpose. As you take time to become more sensitized and educated to great music, your exposure to it will expand your day, bringing you into stronger purpose, greater creativity and follow-through, and clearer vision of your highest goals and ideals for this lifetime.

4

Music for Daily Life

> *If we could devise an arrangement for providing everybody with music in their homes, perfect in quality, unlimited in quantity, suited to every mood, and beginning and ceasing at will, we should consider the limit of human felicity (to be) already attained.*
>
> Edward Bellamy

Your day is now! Every day of your life is important and contains many new opportunities to grow. The more creatively and receptively you can see your lifetime, the less possible it is for you ever to feel bored or defeated.

In order to be ready for as many opportunities as possible, plan and simplify your day. Find the amount of routine necessary for you to feel secure, and how much variety and spontaneity you can handle. Music, appropriately selected, will help you to realize stability, variety and the creative opportunities that you need. Beautiful melodies, carefully chosen according to your daily schedule, will help you to focus and to meet stress with strength. They also will bring into each day a vitality and uplift that enable your life to flow more smoothly.

WAKING UP

It is very unnerving to wake up to a loud alarm clock. It is much more healthy to wake up naturally, with the sun, the sounds of nature, or the melodies of beautiful music. As you sometimes travel far in your sleep, so must you return gradually into your body.

During sleep you can reach into Light—like a great stream of energy emanating from your physical body—to visit, to heal and serve in other places, or to work through a challenge in your own subconscious or unconscious mind. You might have experienced going to another place, often to learn or observe something valuable that can be used later in situations when you are awake. The Bible mentions such "astral projection" through your "silver cord" (Ecclesiastes 12:6). When you return to your physical body, you do not want "to come back in" with a jolt. Therefore, choose wisely the way in which you wake up. Avoid as many shocks to your psyche as possible. Before going to sleep, send out the prayer and invocation that you will wake up at the necessary time each morning. Trust God's guardians and your own awareness to help you in this need.

If this does not work at first, then set a clock radio on a music station that plays beautiful, quiet pieces with melodies that "bring you back" slowly into the new day. Music for strings or flute is especially good. If you are prone to going back to sleep, try music a bit more peppy, but without heavy bass sounds. The tune "Whistle While You Work" is the kind of arouser that will not shock you, yet stirs you enough to get out of bed. Also, Vivaldi's flute concertos and Telemann's string compositions are helpful. They are bright and airy, inviting you joyfully into your new day. Other suggestions would include Prologue to *Sound of Music* and "Morning" from *Peer Gynt* by Grieg.

DAILY GOALS

Each morning scan your day. Perhaps you will find better focus and will accomplish more by making a list of five or six things you want to get done. As you are planning your day, play some music in the background that will clear your mind and direct you toward your desired goals. Play music that will help you to envision all tasks, meetings and projects as going well, in the best order you can conceive.

Here are some musical selections for early morning planning:

> Giuliani - Guitar Concertos
> Vivaldi - Flute Concertos
>   Piccolo Concertos
> Bach, J.S. - Harpsichord Concertos
> Mozart - Clarinet Concerto
>   Concerto for Flute and Harp
> Corelli - Concerti Grossi
> Whistle While You Work
> Prologue from Sound of Music
> When You Wish Upon a Star
> You Light Up My Life
> Oh, What a Beautiful Morning
> Boccherini - Guitar Quintets

Cultivate music in the morning that is joyous and transparent, not heavy or thickly orchestrated; avoid dissonances and crossed harmonies. Keep the music clear, just as you want your own thoughts and energies to be clear and well focused.

MEALS AND GOOD DIGESTION

In his very informative book *The Doctor Prescribes Music*, Dr. Edward Podolsky, a physician, talks about the value of music with our meals. According to him, beautiful music played while we eat aids digestion, actually stimulating the digestive processes and helping them to function better. He mentions a fascinating scientific discovery, that the principal nerve of the tympanum (middle ear) ends in the center of the tongue and connects with the brain, reacting alike to sensations of taste and sound. This is scientific support that good food and good music go together. Music that is pleasing to the ear heightens the taste buds and both work to promote good digestion. It is no accident that in ancient cultures court musicians played while the nobility ate. Even today, beautiful music, such as violin, guitar or harp melodies, played in restaurants, relaxes us, making us feel good and helping our bodily functions to run more smoothly, reacting favorably on glands and nerves.

Dr. Podolsky goes on to describe the opposite effects on our system (p. 82-83):

> Unpleasant emotions bring about certain changes, which give rise to distress. When the stomach is upset, the pylorus (a muscular structure at the base of the stomach) closes. The contents are backed up in the stomach, the organ remains awash and sensations of heaviness, distention and acid risings result. If unpleasant emotions continue to plague the stomach, matters become worse. The person is thus upset and shows drowsiness, mental inefficiency and a tendency to abstraction and day-dreaming. His temper begins to wear thin. He becomes irritable....
>
> Music is the best antidote for unpleasantness at the dinner table. When there is music to be heard, there is an outpouring of gastric juice. This acts as a flushing device. The food is digested properly, it passes from the stomach into the duodenum through a wide-open pylorus.

When choosing music for meals, avoid brass and timpani. Select music that is not heavy or loud; avoid large contrasts, for counter rhythms may interfere with smooth digestion. Choose happy music that is light and airy (especially flute and harp), without deep emotional or intellectual content. Keep your music simple at all meals.

Here are a few suggestions for better eating and digestion:

> Vivaldi - Lute Concertos
>   Oboe Concertos
> Handel - Harp Concerto
>   Flute Sonatas
> Marcello - Sonatas for Recorder
> Mendelssohn - Songs Without Words
>   String Trios
> Grieg - The Last Spring
>   Heart Wounds
>   Piano Concerto (second movement)
>   Holberg Suite
> Koto Flute
> Van Eyck - Music for Recorder
> Mozart - Concerto for Flute and Harp
> Chopin - Piano Concerto No. 1 (second movement)
> Telemann - Table Music

INSOMNIA

Insomnia is a challenge for many persons. You can take sedatives or sleeping pills that often dull your senses, or you can move into sleep creatively. Cultivate quiet, dreamy music for bedtime; avoid late television shows that are either violent or mentally stimulating, and do not eat just before retiring.

As you prepare to go to sleep, first, give thanks to God and offer your day to God in review, with a joyful heart. Release all cares into his keeping for the night of sleep that you need. Prepare yourself even further by selecting a quiet piece of music, for flutes, harps or strings. These sounds will enfold you with soft melodies, which will induce fast and restful sleep. Play just one or two of them before going to sleep. Turn your lights out as you listen. Keep the volume low.

Here is a list of musical selections that will help you to go to sleep quickly and soundly:

Roth - You Are the Ocean
Night Music
Schubert - Ave Maria
Massenet - Meditation (from Thais)
Brahms - Lullaby
Schumann - Traumerei (Dreams)
Debussy - Prelude to the Afternoon of a Faun
  Clair de lune
J.S. Bach - Air on a G String
Palestrina - Pope Marcellus Mass
Pachelbel - Canon in D
Vaughan Williams - Fantasia on a Theme of
  Thomas Tallis
Barber - Adagio for Strings
Humperdinck - Children's Prayer (from Hansel and
  Gretel)

Let these pieces of quiet, melodic music fill you; let them bring you peace, calm and release into the night or daytime of your sleep.

5

cMusic for Home and Family

> *Music touches our innermost being and in that way produces new life, a life that gives exaltation to the whole being, raising it to that perfection in which lies the fulfillment of man's life.*
> Hazrat Inayat Khan

Children, especially very young ones, have come into this incarnation with memory threads of the Kingdoms of Light that they have just left, in order to come to earth. With beautiful music, wisely selected, you can help your child to enter into this lifetime peacefully, with less interruption. And, as a result of the warmer, more loving environment you provide for your children, they will remain more consciously linked with the Eternal Presence that surrounds them. Infants are sensitive to sounds that first enter their psyches. It is wise to avoid as many shocks as possible in today's stress-filled world, both in your own life and in your children's. Just as the warm voice of a caring parent or friend will encourage them, so beautiful music instills hope, confidence to meet challenges, trust and a sense of well-being. It truly makes them feel more at home on earth.

Below are suggestions for different kinds of music that will appeal to different sides of your child's make-up.

QUIET YOUR HOME

Every person and every home needs to balance times of great activity with periods of rest and reflection. This practice helps us find poise and renewal in a busy world. Whenever you feel tension building in yourself or your home, you can use music to help regain the sense of peace and attunement. Cultivate stability and joy by playing some of these musical selections:

Pachelbel - Canon in D
Grainger - Blithe Bells
   Country Gardens
Grieg - Lyric Suite
Mozart - Concerto for Flute and Harp
Telemann - Flute Concerti
   Concerto for Three Violins and Orchestra
James Galway (soloist) - The Magic Flute
   Annie's Song
Gluck - Dance of the Blessed Spirits
Debussy - Clair de lune
Susann McDonald - Miscellaneous Harp Music
Mendelssohn - A Midsummer Night's Dream
Chopin - Polonaises
Tchaikovsky - Waltzes from Sleeping Beauty,
   Swan Lake, Nutcracker
Kreisler-Dvořák - Humoresque

These pieces are especially good as accompaniment to "coming down" after the day's work when loved ones come back together. They are valuable in treating stress, worry and high-strung, emotional states.

It is very therapeutic and intimately lovely to sing to your children, especially at bedtime. This is a way to tell them through music how much they mean to you.

CONSTRUCTIVE ACTIVITY

By now, it should be clear that music falls into three categories:

1. Music that helps you and gives you strength.
2. Music that doesn't do much of anything for you ("blah" music).
3. Music that definitely hurts and weakens you.

How can you tell the difference among these kinds of music? First, you can observe your feelings and responses to the music you experience. Do you feel stronger, happier, more at peace and in tune with life, with persons, with your work, and with your interests? Does your music just bore you? Does your music make you feel tense, agitated, restless, annoyed, angry or violent? Observe how you feel as you listen to your music.

Dr. John Diamond, in his excellent and useful book *Your Body Doesn't Lie*, mentions his investigations into the music children listen to. He says this about the music many children play and parents allow in the home.

> With the rock beat . . ., the entire body is thrown into a state of alarm. The perceptual changes that occur may well manifest themselves in children as decreased performance in school, hyperactivity and restlessness; in adults, as decreased work output, increased errors, general inefficiency, reduced decision-making capacity on the job, and a nagging feeling that things just aren't right—in short the loss of energy for no apparent reason. This has been observed clinically hundreds of times. In my practice I have found that the academic records of many schoolchildren improve considerably after they stop listening to rock music while studying.

The rock beat seriously hampers energy flow, and it distorts the senses, mental abilities and spiritual attunement. I recall tutoring a boy who was having severe nervous problems, both in school and at home. He responded very strongly and positively to the soothing melodies of Dvořák's "Largo" (from his Symphony No. 9) and was able to do his homework much more easily and creatively. He also said that this piece calmed him down, while a trumpet concerto by Haydn enabled him "to think straighter." (Incidentally this former rock lover really enjoyed Haydn.) This incident proved to me again that good work is enhanced by the sounds of beautiful, harmonious music.

Stimulating the Imagination. Many examples of great music are dramatic in a particularly descriptive way. Sometimes this music has been called program music, for it is music with a story—music that paints a story with sound. Such music can help you and your child to release more imagination. It can stimulate you to paint pictures inwardly with your power of visualization. You may find fantasies and dreams coming alive, thus awakening greater creative outlet and expression. Such music energizes and inspires you in your work, in relationships, and in your recreation.

These selections are good antidotes for a passive consciousness, especially helpful for children and adults who might tend to be slaves of television and other machines. Much of this music has been used in films and shows, since it is colorful and stimulating to the imagination.

You might want to listen to these pieces with your eyes closed or with a notebook by your side, to jot down impressions and pictures that come to mind:

> Mozart - Piano Concerto No. 21
> Beethoven - Symphony No. 6 (Pastorale)
> Smetana - The High Castle
>   Moldau
> Liszt - Hungarian Rhapsodies
> Dvořák - Slavonic Dances
> Hovhaness - And God Created Great Whales
> Britten - Four Sea Interludes (from Peter Grimes)
> Delius - Florida Suite
> Copland - Lincoln Portrait
>   Quiet City
>   Appalachian Spring
> Bloch - Schelomo
> Berlioz - Harold in Italy

Ravel - Daphnis and Chloe (Suite No. 2)
Ketelbey - Bells Across the Meadow
    In a Monastery Garden
Haydn - Creation

RELEASE YOUR CHILD'S ENERGY

Your children deserve to be bathed in beautiful, melodic music—the best that you can find for them. Particularly when they are very young, you should avoid playing stressful, clashing sounds. As they get older, you will find that music with a more defined rhythm can help to direct and motivate their energies.

Certain beautiful and very rhythmical music, like a Haydn symphony, will often help them to concentrate in their homework, while other chaotic sounds will make them lose concentration and will make them jumpy, even when they do not have work to do.

Here is some music that will stimulate your children of three years and older without attacking them or causing them to feel fragmented and confused:

Villa-Lobos - Little Train of the Caipira (from
    Bachianas Brasileiras No. 2)
Anderson - Sleigh Ride
    The Typewriter
    Syncopated Clock
Delibes - Coppelia
Tchaikovsky - Nutcracker
Saint Saens - Carnival of the Animals
Grainger - Lincolnshire Posy
    Country Gardens
Mendelssohn - A Midsummer Night's Dream
Ponchielli - Dance of the Hours
Dukas - The Sorcerer's Apprentice
Hovhaness - Sinbad the Sailor
Dohnanyi - Variations on a Nursery Song
Poulenc - Story of Babar the Elephant
Diamond - Jonathan Livingston Seagull

Soundtracks: The Sound of Music; Mary Poppins;
  Snow White and the Seven Dwarfs; Fantasia;
  Winnie the Pooh; Sleeping Beauty; Cinderella
Haydn - Toy Symphony
Beethoven, Mozart - German Dances
Prokofiev - Peter and the Wolf
Harsanyi - Story of the Little Tailor
Ravel - Mother Goose Suite
  L'Enfant et les sortileges
Rimsky-Korsakov - Scheherazade
Tubby the Tuba
Hans Christian Anderson
Seeger - Songs for Children
For a Child's Heart
Offenbach - Gaité Parisienne
Winter - Common Ground
Collins - Whales and Nightingales
Joseph's Technicolor Dream Coat
Walton - For Children
Shostakovich - Polka (from Age of Gold)
Hopkins - John and the Magic Music Man

See Appendix for further suggestions.

OTHER LANDS AND THE PAST

Throughout the land today, in spite of stress, increasing
polarities and even the prophets of doom, many persons
sense a new breakthrough in consciousness already on the
horizon. This is the coming "New Age," or Age of
Aquarius, which, according to higher teachings, will promote a fuller expression of the brotherhood of mankind. It
will also emphasize greater interdependence of persons
freely sharing their good with others, a cooperative group
effort toward peace and jointly constructive goals, scientific advances, creative synthesis in the arts, and greater international harmony and communication.

Above all, our times are revealing to us how precious
and valuable each life is, since in some way each of us con-

tributes to the whole. By working together, we come to feel a greater reverence for life and by helping others we open new pathways of service, recognizing more clearly our place as a receptor and channel in God's unfolding universe.

In the midst of this expanding consciousness and global communication, it is important to awaken in your child a growing awareness and appreciation for *all* cultures and nations, to help your child (and yourself) to experience other peoples, cultures and traditions, so as to develop a more universal perspective. Music can help you to move in this direction. As various media can take viewers on trips to many lands, so can music awaken deep feelings, past, present and future, of many places and races on this planet.

While appreciating your own particular, national heritage and background, you can use the following musical pieces to help your child become a planetary citizen. As you share such music with your children, try to show accompanying pictures of lands and peoples, perhaps from *National Geographic Magazine* or other travel periodicals and history books. These pieces need some introduction.

Do not play them too often. Blend such music into your home environment appropriately, for example, at certain holiday celebrations.

The *Nonesuch Explorer* series of recordings is an excellent way to travel around the world, musically.

> *Celtic Lands:* Stivell - Renaissance of the Celtic
>   Harp
> *Mayan and Incan:* Harp Music of the Andes
>   Chants and Songs of Yma Sumac
> *England and Ireland:* Music of Vaughan Williams
>   (especially Oxford Elegy and To a Lark
>   Ascending)
>   Danny Boy (sung by Robert White)
>   Music of the Chieftains; Boys of the Lough

Scotland: Bagpipe music and songs of Calum
   Kennedy
France: Offenbach - Gaité Parisienne
   Zamfir - Flute of Pan
   Milhaud - Suite Provençale
India: Ragas played by Ravi Shankar or Ali
   Akhabar Khan
Russia: Osipov Balalaika Orchestra (Russian folk
   music)
   Rachmaninoff - Vespers, Liturgy of St. John
   Chrysostom
Japan: Music for the Koto
   Kimio Eto plays the koto
   Hovhaness - Fantasy on Japanese Woodprints
   Galway - Song of the Seashore
   Music for Zen Meditation
China: Yellow River Concerto
   Music for the Chinese Classical Orchestra
Germany: Music of Old Vienna (conductor, Willi
   Boskovsky)
   Schumann - Symphony No. 1 (Spring)
Austria: Johann Strauss - Waltzes
Roumania: Georges Enesco - Roumanian
   Rhapsodies
   Gypsy Melodies
Italy: Gioacchino Rossini - Overtures
   Luciano Pavarotti - arias and Neapolitan Songs
Spain: Joaquin Rodrigo - Concierto de Aranjuez
Scandinavia: Music of Edvard Grieg
   Jean Sibelius,
   Christian Sinding
Hawaii: Songs of the Islands, such as Hawaiian
   Wedding Song
   Songs sung by Alfred Alpaka
Israel: Kol Nidrei, Hebrew Cantorial Songs,
   Shalom, Sacred Service
   Ernest Bloch - Israel Symphony
   Schelomo (Solomon)
Greece: Bouzouki Music - Theodorakis (Le Chant
   du Monde)

Mexico: Music played by Mariachi bands
Africa: David Fanshawe - African Sanctus
  Misa Luba
South America: Misa Criolla
  Los Calchakis
United States: American Indian - Kaibah (Navaho
  songs), Hopi Butterfly
  Paul Robeson - Negro Spirituals
  American Civil War - Songs of the North and
  South (Mormon Tabernacle Choir)
Australia and New Zealand: Lilburn - Symphony
  No. 2, Aotearoa Overture
  From New Zealand with Love
  Maori Songs, St. Joseph Choir

MAGIC OF THE ORCHESTRA

What is more beautiful than a lovely moment in nature, a deep friendship, or the sounds of a hundred-piece orchestra making music! One of the greatest gifts you can give your children is to acquaint them with the subtle flavors, tones and essences of the different instruments of the orchestra. As you take time to play for them, either "live" or with recordings, observe what sounds, rhythms, melodies and harmonies move them most. You can recognize their needs more clearly, as you learn to sense their musical tastes.

Here are some basic selections to help you go through the whole orchestra with your child:

Britten - Young Person's Guide to the Orchestra
  (with narrator)
Saint Saens - Carnival of the Animals
The Instruments of the Orchestra (narrated by Sir
  Adrian Boult)
The Instruments of the Orchestra, by David
  Randolph
Invitation to Music (narrated by Elie Siegmeister)
John and the Magic Music Man - Child's Guide to
  the Orchestra, by A. Hopkins

Brass: The brass instruments stimulate the physical body. They are very powerful and arouse feelings of nobility, potency, majesty, but at times can give a sense of terror. Too much brass music at once can prove disturbing.

> *Trumpets:* Bruckner - Symphony No. 9
>   Wagner - Overture to Die Meistersinger
> *Horns:* Mozart - Horn Concertos
>   Britten - Serenade for Tenor, Horn and
>   Strings
> *Trombone:* Walker - Trombone Concerto
>   Mozart - Requiem (Tuba Mirum)
> *Tuba:* Mussorgsky - Bydlo (Ox Wagon) from
>   Pictures at an Exhibition
>   Sibelius - Symphony No. 2 (finale)
> *Cornets:* Debussy - La Mer
> *Saxhorn:* Mahler - Symphony No. 7 (opening)

Percussion: The percussion instruments also stimulate the physical body. These instruments are struck; they add rhythm, color and sound-power to the orchestral texture. Like the brass, these instruments must be added into the work with good taste and proportion. (Avoid "over-spicing" with percussion.)

> *Kettledrums:* Handel oratorios and Bach cantatas
>   Beethoven - Symphony No. 9
> *Snare drum:* Shostakovich - Symphony No. 5
> *Tambourine:* Tchaikovsky - Arab Dance (from
>   Nutcracker)
> *Triangle:* Respighi - Pines of Rome
> *Cymbals:* Tchaikovsky - Symphony No. 4 (finale)
> *Gong:* Respighi - Pines of Rome (Catacombs
>   movement)
>   Tchaikovsky - Symphony No. 6 (finale)
> *Castanets:* Debussy - Iberia
> *Glockenspiel:* Vaughan Williams - Symphony No. 8
> *Xylophone:* Saint Saens - Dance Macabre
> *Vibraphone:* Britten - Spring Symphony (opening
>   section)

Tubular bells: Tchaikovsky - 1812 Overture
Celesta: Bartok - Music for Strings, Percussion and
   Celesta
Anvil: Verdi - Anvil Chorus (from Il Trovatore)
Marimba: Creston - Concertino for Marimba and
   Orchestra
Wind machine: Vaughan Williams - Symphony
   No. 7 (Antarctica)

Woodwinds: The woodwinds maintain the melodic line, and they bring out the more airy, transparent quality of the orchestral sound. The woodwinds will affect the emotions and feelings primarily. They can make you feel lighter and clearer.

Flute: Bach - Suite in B-minor
   Mozart - Concerto for Flute and Harp
Piccolo: Vivaldi - Piccolo Concertos
Oboe: Mozart - Concerto for Oboe
   R. Thompson - Suite for Oboe, Clarinet and
   Viola
English horn: Sibelius - Swan of Tuonela
   Copland - Quiet City
Clarinet: Rachmaninoff - Symphony No. 2 (slow
   movement)
Bass clarinet: Stravinsky - Petrouchka
Bassoon: Dukas - Sorcerer's Apprentice
Double bassoon: Ravel - Piano Concerto for Left
   Hand (opening)
Saxophone: Glazounov - Concerto for Saxophone

Strings: The strings soothe you, calm you and bring a feeling of harmony and peace. They will appeal more to your mind and to your soul, as they remind you of continuity and eternal music of the spheres.

Violin: Beethoven - Violin Concerto
   Mendelssohn - Violin Concerto
Cello: Dvořák - Cello Concerto
   Villa-Lobos - Fantasia Concertante
Viola: Berlioz - Harold in Italy
   Walton - Viola Concerto

Double bass: Mahler - Symphony No. 1 (funeral
   march)
Harp: Sibelius - The Bard
   Bruckner - Symphony No. 8 (3d movement)
   Hanson - Concerto for Organ, Strings and Harp
   Handel - Harp Concerto in F
Guitar: Rodrigo - Concierto de Aranjuez
   Fantasy for a Courtier
Mandolin: Mahler - Symphony No. 7
Strings in total: Bach - Brandenburg Concertos

Organ: This instrument, called "king of instruments,"
brings in great power and connection with the celestial
music of the spheres. Some organ pieces are especially
uplifting to the soul.

Bach: Come Sweet Death (as played by Virgil Fox)
Franck: Prière; Three Chorales
Saint Saens: Symphony No. 3 (Organ)
Jongen: Symphonie Concertante for Organ and
   Orchestra

See Appendix for a list of other pieces for children.

Electronic:
Dexter - Golden Voyage I; III
Carlos - Switched on Bach

Sounds of Nature:
Songs of the Humpbacked Whale, Vols. I & II
Environments Recordings

Harmonizing Melodies:
Schubert - Rosamunde: Incidental Music
Toning by Laurel Keys (*see* Bibliography)

WEDDINGS

Weddings are very beautiful, intimate occasions. They
are often attended by great Presences and spiritual power.
Good friends emanate love and warm wishes for a harmonious and productive marriage. As the ceremony

begins, power builds. Beautiful music attunes the participants and sets the tone for the whole service.

Perhaps during the ceremony the couple will want a favorite piece of spiritual music sung or played. Later, a stirring recessional melody fills everyone with a sense of finality and a promise of unity in the future. The postlude allows all who are attending to "come down" again into the present, bringing new joy and dedication into their own relationships.

Very often we feel the power of angelic presences who seal the couple in auric union during their vows. Given the spiritual significance of marriage, it is important to choose the music wisely. Harsh vibrations and all raucous music should be carefully avoided. Pleasing, flowing melodies, especially if played on an organ bring majesty and reverence into the ceremony. A harp fills the atmosphere with a lifting transparency of sound, thus opening doors to higher Presences attending. Strings provide clarity to the feelings and thoughts of the participants.

Here are some suggestions for music at weddings:

Preludes:

> Grieg - Morning (from Peer Gynt)
> > The Last Spring
> > I Love Thee
> Rachmaninoff - Love Theme (18th Variation - from Rhapsody on a Theme of Paganini)
> Elgar - Nimrod Variation (from Enigma Variations)
> Mascagni - Intermezzo (from Cavalleria Rusticana)
> Allen - Celebration for Harp
> Massenet - Meditation (from Thais)
> Schubert - Ave Maria
> Bach-Gounod - Ave Maria
> Liszt - Liebestraum
> Wagner - Prelude and Love-Death (from Tristan und Isolde)
> Debussy - Clair de lune

Bach - Sheep May Safely Graze
Herbert - Ah, Sweet Mystery of Life
Streisand - Evergreen

Processionals:

Wagner - Wedding March (from Lohengrin)
Rodgers and Hammerstein - Wedding Processional
(from Sound of Music)
Schmidt - Intermezzo (from Notre Dame)
Clarke - Trumpet Voluntary

Recessionals:

Mendelssohn - Wedding March (from A Midsummer Night's Dream)
Rodgers and Hammerstein - Alleluia (from Sound of Music)
Climb Every Mountain (from Sound of Music)
Rheinberger - Organ Concertos (E. Power Biggs)

Miscellaneous Wedding Music:

D'Hardelot - Because
This Moment Divine
Bond - I Love You Truly
DeKoven - O Promise Me
A Wedding Prayer
Denver, Domingo - Perhaps Love
Cooke - Love Sends a Little Gift of Roses
Friml - L'Amour, Toujours L'Amour
Lehar - Yours Is My Heart Alone
Goss - Praise My Soul
Youmans-Heyman - Through the Years
Parry - Bridal March
Haydn - St. Anthony Chorale (Virgil Fox on Organ)
An especially beautiful, spiritually oriented wedding song in a contemporary, melodic vein is
"There Is Love," composed by Captain and Tennille.

BIRTH

We come from Light, and we return into Light. The great opposites of life are birth and death, not life and death.

As a mother conceives and begins to build a foetus for the soul attracted into incarnation through her, it is very important to cultivate a beautiful atmosphere for the incoming life. The home environment that is clean, lovely, with bright colors and paintings will allow Light to permeate the household, through the windows and through the consciousness of the householders.

Again, lovely music can help to prepare the way for the incoming child, and it heightens the atmosphere in the home. Here are some calming, welcoming pieces that will help the infant to enter earth's density in joy and warmth:

> Van Eyck - Music for Recorder
> Saint Saens - The Swan (from Carnival of the Animals)
> Humperdinck - Children's Prayer (from Hansel and Gretel)
> Massenet - Meditation (from Thais)
> Wolf-Ferrari - Intermezzo (from Secret of Suzanne)
> Fauré - Requiem (In Paradiso)
> Brahms - Lullaby
> Debussy - Clair de lune
> J.S. Bach - Air on a G String
> Handel - Largo (from Xerxes)
> Braga - Angels' Serenade
> Miscellaneous Harp Music (especially Nicanor Zabaleta, soloist)
> Mozart - Piano Concerto No. 21 (2nd movement)
> Wagner - Evening Star (from Tannhauser)
> Gluck - Dance of the Blessed Spirits
> Grieg - Holberg Suite
> Jean-Pierre Rampal (miscellaneous flute music)
> Dexter - Golden Voyage I, III
> Koto Flute
> Lullaby from the Womb, Dr. Hajime Murooka

TRANSITION

When our time comes, we take leave of our bodies to return into God's greater mansions of Light. There is individual continuity; just our cloak (the physical body) is left behind. As we make our transition, again we want the kind of musical accompaniment that blends with Silence and clears our entrance into celestial Light.

At a passing and at a memorial service, it is essential to play music that will sound vibrations of joyful release and a smooth journey over to the other side, where angels, loved ones and great messengers of Light await us. Let joyful music ring out toward the beautiful, unlimited horizons of God's luminous habitations, prepared for us.

Whatever music you choose for a person's passing, select melodies that inspire, lift and lighten the atmosphere. The loved one's passing should be a time of great joy, as he finds release into a much larger, more beautiful dimension of life. Play music that celebrates the loved one's transition as a true graduation and victory. Avoid at all costs any music that is sorrowful, heavy-laden or artificially sentimental: the veil between this world and the next is very thin.

At any passing and memorial service, let us choose music that supports these thoughts, written by a spiritual teacher, the Reverend Flower A. Newhouse, in her book *Speak The Word* (p. 88):

> Life is endless, deathless, inexhaustible, and eternal. It becomes ever more purposeful, refined, and majestic as our grades are approached and completed. Eventually, the Earth will have nothing more to teach us, so there shall be no necessity for our return.
>
> Realizing all this, we . . . release _____, not into death, but into the sublime consciousness of a freer, fuller, and happier life. Our thoughts and prayers shall follow _____ wherever he / she journeys, for in God there is no division of

existence, and we dwell not in other worlds as much as upon other levels of awareness.

Here are some suggestions of music to play at one's passing and at the memorial service:

Schubert - Ave Maria
R. Strauss - Death and Transfiguration (closing section)
Humperdinck - Children's Prayer (from Hansel and Gretel)
Wagner - Pilgrim's Chorus
    Prelude and Good Friday Spell (from Parsifal)
C. Bohm - Calm As the Night (organ)
Bach-Fox - Come Sweet Death (organ)
Fauré - Requiem (In Paradise)
Herbert - Ah, Sweet Mystery of Life
Elgar - Pomp and Circumstance
Schmidt - Intermezzo (from Notre Dame)
Rodgers-Hammerstein - Climb Every Mountain (from Sound of Music)
Mendelssohn - Selections from Elijah
Brahms - How Lovely Is Thy Dwelling Place (from a German Requiem)
Grieg - Piano Concerto (2d movement)

O you my God, your mercy has left prayer to us as a connection, a blessed connection with you: as a blessing which gives us more than all fulfillment.   Arnold Schoenberg

HUMOR IN MUSIC

Sometimes music is simply good for a laugh, allowing a happy, fun-filled opportunity for release. Norman Cousins, in his helpful book *The Anatomy of an Illness*, points out the therapeutic value of good, genuine laughter, for it will untie knots in the emotions, in the mind and body, and it opens the whole system to the inpouring energies of the universe. Humor is an important ventilating device, and there is much good music that will help you to unwind with a chuckle.

Here is a short list of some musical pieces that are filled with good humor and pleasing spirits:

> Irish jigs
> Scottish reels
> Tchaikovsky - Dance of the Sugar Plum Fairy
> (from the Nutcracker Suite)
> Victor Borge - Comedy in Music
> Anna Russell, musical parodies
> Haydn - Toy Symphony
> Mozart - A Musical Joke
> J.S. Bach - Suites for Orchestra
> R. Strauss - Till Eulenspiegel's Merry Pranks
> Grainger - Handel in the Strand and Others
> Gilbert and Sullivan
> Hoffnung Concerts
> I'm Gonna Wash That Man Right Out of My Hair,
> from South Pacific
> Beauty and the Beast and Snow White and the
> Seven Dwarfs
> Walt Disney recordings for children, especially
> Bambi, Dumbo, Mary Poppins, Winnie the
> Pooh
> When You Wish Upon a Star

Learn to laugh more in life and to see the fun in situations, persons and opportunities. More important, learn to laugh at yourself, for it will bring you freedom and possibilities for defusing that will not only be enjoyable but essential to your health.

6

The Music of Nature

*I have learned my songs from the music of
many birds, from the music of many waters.*

The Kalevala

Music and nature are two outstanding pathways into
God's expanding Light. If you become more reverent and
sensitive toward all that lives and the wonders of creation,
you will feel new openings, leading you more deeply into
the Divine Presence. If you show greater care and kindness
toward animals, trees and the environments of nature, you
will feel more strongly how closely you are attended and
nourished by many higher Presences who look after your
welfare.

Increase your attunement to nature by refining these
areas:

1. Feel more love and appreciation for all lives surround-
ing you.

2. Increase study and acquaintance with nature. For example, read articles from *National Geographic Magazine*,
the works of Edwin Way Teale, J. Muir, Thoreau, H.
Beston, J. Krutch; the poetry of Frost, R. Jeffers. Take
walks into nature, sitting quietly in the woods and reading
about the presences in nature—in books like *The Journey
Upward* by F. A. Newhouse; *The Kingdom of the Gods* by

Geoffrey Hodson. Study the laws of nature as described in *The Seven Mysteries of Life* by Guy Murchie, and *The Beautiful Necessity* by Claude Bragdon, and the ways of nature in *The Findhorn Garden*, *The Tao of Physics* (scientific) by F. Capra, and *The Symphony of Life* by D. Andrews.

3. Listen continuously to great music of nature.

4. Meditate creatively on the mysteries and presences of nature.

5. Get out into nature, using all your senses and perception to experience its majesty.

So many simple joys and pleasures are extended from nature: the fragrances of pine trees, the colors and combined shadings of flowers growing side by side, the songs and cries of birds; the cool, damp vitality of soil held in the hands; the shapes and energy of stones; the rippling rhythms of a stream or lake; the eternity in song of an ocean. Notice these simple gifts of God, appreciate them each day in your life. Take full advantage of the joys and gifts in nature, for these will continuously help to balance and harmonize you in all the layers of your consciousness.

Certain composers have been especially sensitive to the harmonies and sounding essences of nature. Often these great tone painters have heard the calls of mountain, sea and forest presences, and they have been able to blend with them closely. Such composers channel these calls into notes and melodies on musical instruments.

It is interesting to see how some composers have tried to imitate the sounds and melodies of nature, (for example, Beethoven's "Pastoral" Symphony; or Respighi's "Pines of Rome," while others, such as Scriabin and Hovhaness, have tried to bring through active deva (nature-angel) music and the sympathetic resonance of nature's soundings. Sometimes a great piece of nature music will sound more elfin or humanized to our ears (Grieg's "Nocturne" or Vivaldi's *Four Seasons*), while other nature music will sound awesome and untamed, like forces in a primeval forest or savage ocean powers (Sibelius's "Tapiola," "The Tempest," or Symphony No. 4). The music of nature is unending in its variety and contrasts.

Here is a list of various pieces of nature music and a few suggestive comments about what to look for as you listen to them. Each area of the world has its own distinctive musical characteristics, as the world of nature is different in each.

NORTH AMERICA

The greatest American music is fresh and alive, containing a vitality and spirit unlike any other. Beethoven said, "One must go to North America to give free vent to one's ideas." It is this sense of freedom and the vision of a new frontier—in nature and in consciousness—which make much American music unique. The following composers and pieces are suggestive of nature pictorially described in music. Label numbers are included as these pieces are not repeated in the Appendix.

> Edward MacDowell - Woodland Sketches, Sea Pieces, Fireside Tales, New England Idylls (Columbia AML 4372)
> Suite No. 1, Suite No. 2 (Indian), (Mercury 75026)
> To a Wild Rose (Columbia M30066)
> Two piano concertos (various labels)

MacDowell's music is refined nature music, suggesting to me various scenes and movements of nature and the four elements—beautifully melodic and at times very impressionistic.

> Frederick Delius - Florida Suite (Seraphim S-60212)
> Appalachia (Angel S-36756)

Delius synthesized five major influences: German, Scandinavian, French, English and American. The *Florida Suite* suggests to me early American scenes in Florida at night among the orange groves, where Delius stayed for a time tending his father's property. I really like the atmospheric combination of the sounds of nature at night and sounds of old Negro spirituals, moving on the waters.

Appalachia, from the same place, also suggests movements in nature, combining with the longings and feelings of a trek with sorrows—a journey of joys and hardships.

Roy Harris - Symphony No. 3 (Columbia MS-6303)
    Symphony No. 5 (Louisville S-655)
    Symphonies No. 1, 7 (Columbia MS-5095)
To me the music of Roy Harris suggests the marvelous, relentless beauty of the Midwestern plains. I feel so often in this music the essential American spirit of freedom, the glory of labor, the sinewy, muscular quality in people, sounding through the reaping of stalks of corn and "amber waves of grain."

Harris uses the brass in his works to great advantage, to me suggesting the blaze of sun on soil and the sounds of bugles and horns reaching to new horizons. I find Harris's music unique for its spirit, its activating rhythms, and its strength in movement. It's powerful but not always therapeutic.

Howard Hanson - Symphony No. 1 (Nordic), No. 3
    (Mercury 75112)
    Symphony No. 2 (Romantic) (Mercury 75007)
Hanson's music for me is melodic and powerful, suggesting both the ancient bards and forests of Scandinavia and the northern woodlands of America. Note the very beautiful slow movement of Symphony No. 2, which takes us deep into forests and woods, only to emerge into a full, panoramic view of watery ocean and mountain peaks.

Charles Ives - The Pond (Columbia MS-7318)
    Symphony No. 3 (Mercury 75035)
    Symphony No. 4 (Columbia MS-6775)
    Three Places in New England (DGG 2530048)
Ives's music, for me, is a fascinating combination of rugged good humor, intercrossing tunes, complex rhythms and a Yankee temperament that is everything from feisty and brittle to warm and romantic. The pieces suggested above

bring out Ives's sensitivity to nature, which the composer appreciated deeply during his long life in New England. His music is many-faceted, not always pleasant, but compelling. It suggests the ambience of New England nature scenes—the sun, cloudy rain days, the gold and gray of life in all its changing moods.

The genius of Ives's works, I believe, is his ability to picture musically the great polarities of life and the human condition—the cold and warm, the heat and snow—mingled together in such scenes as the festive celebrations of villagers and old time bands approaching, passing by and leaving fallen gravestones in forgotten cemeteries; and the watching eyes of ponds, echoing in the night. Enter into Ive's music with openness, imagination, and the ability to laugh at everything, even yourself. His music, however, is rarely therapeutic.

Samuel Barber - Music for a Scene from Shelley; Essay No. 2 for Orchestra; Serenade for String Orchestra (Vanguard 2083)
Adagio for Strings (Columbia MS-6224)
Violin Concerto (Columbia MS-6713)

For me, much of Barber's music has a fresh, lyrical quality often suggesting wild, beautiful landscapes. Many of his works are inspired by poetry and literature of nature and the human condition.

Alan Hovhaness - Mysterious Mountain (RCA LSC-2251)
Mountains and Rivers without End (Poseidon 1004)
Talin (Peters PLE-071)

The music of Hovhaness for me is a unique synthesis of East-West. I feel a strong Oriental quality in much of his work and also a strong flavor of Armenian liturgical music and an American lyricism. At its finest, Hovhaness's pieces reveal private worlds of spiritual mysticism, with crystalline grottos, moonlit gardens, and spacious heights. The vision of universal brotherhood permeates many of his works, especially Symphony No. 10 (*All Men Are Brothers*).

Rodgers and Hammerstein - The Sound of Music (RCA LSOD-2005)

The Prologue, "Climb Every Mountain," and "Edelweiss" sections of this soundtrack contain very beautiful and powerful nature music. In these uplifting melodies the composer has captured the sounds of mountain devas and presences calling to each other. Each peak echoes its own unique "tones" as mountains sing out in joy, sending forth strong beams of Light and healing energies that fill the listener and atmosphere. Other selections of nature music include:

Ferde Grofé - Grand Canyon Suite, Sunset (Columbia MS-6618)

Charles T. Griffes - Poem for Flute and Orchestra (Mercury 75020)
White Peacock; Clouds (Mercury SR1-75090)

Virgil Thomson - The River; Plow that Broke the Plains (Vanguard 2095)
Sea Piece with Birds (CR1-398)

Thomas Canning - Fantasy on Hymn of Justin Morgan (Everest 3070)

ENGLAND, SCOTLAND AND WALES

There is nothing quite so winsome and appealing as an English pastoral scene—so serene, clear and filled with presences in nature and alive with guardian beings. Many English composers were also particularly attuned to nature and were able to bring through musically the whisperings of woodland presences and the powerful energies moving among fields, trees, mountains and sea. Here are just a few of them:

Ralph Vaughan Williams - Lark Ascending (Angel S-36902)
In the Fen Country (Angel S-36902)
Symphony No. 3 (Pastoral) (RCA LSC-3281)
Symphony No. 5 (Angel S-35952)
Symphony No. 7 (Antarctic) (Angel S-36763)

To me, the music of Vaughan Williams always represents a strong emotional-spiritual experience, processed and polished through the mind into a refined and complete art form. I feel in this composer's music a rustic and mystical quality that has been synthesized by a wise, urbane consciousness, bringing the result of a shining, though seemingly effortless art form. I have always felt uplifted by his greatest nature pieces. There is a vision and a grandeur to them which sweeps the listener along, and portrays nobility and faith's upward reach of the heart.

George Butterworth - Two English Idylls, The Banks of Green Willow, A Shropshire Lad (Argo ZRG-860)

Butterworth is a nature tone poet of first rank. He was killed in World War I, at a tragically young age. His nature scenes for me are beautiful and clear, suggesting a yearning toward immortality amidst the trees, streams and fields. The listener is alone in nature, but always accompanied by invisible presences that breathe all around him. An idyllic, faerie-filled atmosphere pervades Butterworth's music.

Gerald Finzi - A Severn Rhapsody, Nocturne, The Fall of the Leaf (HNH 4077)
Earth and Air and Rain (Argo ZRG-838)

Finzi's music is removed and solitary, but also paints beautiful nature scenes. It suggests the joy of immortality and the sorrows of earthly transience.

Frederick Delius - Summer Evening (Seraphim S-60000)
Over the Hills and Far Away (Seraphim S-60212)
In a Summer Garden (Angel S-36588)
Summer Night on the River (Angel S-36588)
Song of the High Hills (Angel S-37011)
On Hearing the First Cuckoo in Spring (Seraphim S-60185)
A Song of Summer (Angel S-36415)
Song Before Sunrise (Argo ZRG-875)

Delius's nature music is more suggestive than directly pictorial. It is as though Delius takes us inside nature, to penetrate its atmosphere more than to describe it literally.

For this reason Delius's music requires repeated listening and the ability to flow inside its harmonies and tonal qualities. Give ear and mind and heart to Delius's music, and you will enter worlds and atmospheres filled with nature beings.

> Sir Arnold Bax - The Garden of Fand, Tintagel (HNH 4034)
> The seven Symphonies (Lyrita Records)

With the music of Sir Arnold Bax you will be taken into the untamed reaches of nature. Scenes of craggy coasts, storms in the forests and nature beings will open up to you. Listen to Bax at night and you may well wish to have someone in the room with you, for his tone poems are often awesome and very powerful, but rarely therapeutic.

> Ernest Moeran - Symphony; Lonely Waters (EMI / HMV-CSD 3705)

> Benjamin Britten - Four Sea Interludes (from Peter Grimes) (Angel S-36215)

> John Ireland - Concertino Pastorale (Musical Heritage 1498H)
> A Downland Suite (Musical Heritage 1498H)

> Sir Edward Elgar - Sea Pictures (Angel S-36796)
> Percy Grainger - Music of Grainger (Mercury 75102) (EMI - EMD-5514)

> Sir Arthur Bliss - Miracle in the Gorbals (EMI ASD 3342)

> Hadley - The Hills (EMI - Odeon SAN393)

FRANCE

French music of nature is marked by two chief qualities: light, transparent textures and drama. As a general rule, French music is not as heavy as English. Sometimes it is filled with spicy, humorous sounds.

Here are some of the best pieces of French music of nature:

Achille Claude Debussy - La Mer (London STS 15109
   or RCA VICS-1041)
   Nocturnes (Columbia M-30483)
   Prelude to the Afternoon of a Faun (RCA VICS-1323)
   Sacred and Profane Dances (Columbia MS-7362)
   The Engulfed Cathedral (London 21006)
   Images (Columbia MS-7362)
   Miscellaneous piano music

Debussy's music is mysterious and echoes another
world—a world of nymphs and naiads, water devas and
sirens of the deep. A feeling of worlds under water, such as
the lost kingdom of Atlantis, are strongly felt in "The
Engulfed Cathedral," which rises from the deep, only to
sink again into total submersion.

César Franck - Piano Quintet (RCA LSC-2739)
Franck's music is, for me, angelic. According to Cyril Scott
in his book *Music: Its Secret Influence Through the Ages*,
Franck's music forms a bridge between humans and devas.

Vincent D'Indy - Symphony on a French Mountain
   Air (Odyssey Y-31274)
   The Enchanted Forest; Summer Day
   (Arabesque-8097-2)

Joseph Canteloube - Songs of the Auvergne (Angel
   S-36897, S-36898)

Hector Berlioz - Fantastic Symphony, 3d movement:
   Scenes in the Country (Angel S-37485)

Francis Poulenc - Rustic Concerto for Harpsichord
   and Orchestra, especially the slow movement.
   (Angel S-35993)

Maurice Ravel - Daphnis and Chloe (RCA AGL
   1-1270)
   A Ship on the Ocean (Angel S-37150)
   Miscellaneous piano music

Darius Milhaud - Suite Provençale (RCA
   AGL1-2445)

Ernest Chausson - Poem of Love and the Sea (Angel
   S-36897)
   Symphony in B-Flat (Seraphim S-60310)

SOUTH AMERICA AND SPAIN

While there are many South American composers and many noteworthy works from them, I find few that take the listener into nature's realms. Among those are these:

> Heitor Villa-Lobos (Brazil) - Forest of the Amazon
> (United Artists UAS 8007)
> Bachianas Brasileiras, Nos. 2, 5, 6, 9 (Angel 35547)
> Mystic Sextet (Musical Heritage 3397)
> Origin of the Amazon River (Columbia AML 4615)

Sadly, the powerful, exotic and haunting music of this erratic genius has been too much neglected. Villa-Lobos's music is unlike any other—folkish, yet serious, at times intensely dramatic, always melodic and compelling. His scenes of nature recall lost waterfalls within wild, exotic jungles of South America; haunting melodies of love and battle; always exciting, sometimes profound.

> Manuel deFalla (Spain) - Nights in the Gardens of Spain (RCA LSC-2430)

> Alberto Ginastera (Argentina) - Symphony No. 3 (Pampeana) (Louisville 545-10)

> Joaquin Rodrigo (Spain) - Concierto de Aranjuez, slow movement (Turnabout 34636)

> E. Salvador Bacarisse (Spain) - Guitar Concerto, slow movement (DGG-2530326)

GERMANY AND AUSTRIA

Many composers have left us beautiful music suggesting the Rhineland scenes of nature. The German-Austrian tradition usually offers music that is thickly orchestrated, often memorably melodic. Each of the following composers has brought through certain pieces of music which strongly suggest nature's harmonies. Here are some of them:

> Ludwig van Beethoven - Symphony No. 6 (Pastoral) (Angel S-35711)

Felix Mendelssohn - A Midsummer Night's Dream
(London STS-15084)
Symphony No. 4 (Italian) (Philips 9500068)

Robert Schumann - Symphony No. 1 (Spring) (Angel
S-36353)

Johannes Brahms - Symphony No. 2 (Columbia
M-35129) (London STS-15192)

Gustav Mahler - Symphony Nos. 3, 4, 6, 7
(miscellaneous labels)

Anton Bruckner - Symphony No. 4 (Romantic)
(DGG 2535111)

Richard Strauss - An Alpine Symphony (London
6981)
From Italy (Seraphim S-60301)

Richard Wagner - Forest Murmurs (Angel S-35947)
Dawn and Siegfried's Rhine Journey (2London
STS-15251 / 2)
Ride of the Valkyries (London 21016)

SCANDINAVIA

Equally compelling in its own way is the pictorial music
of nature composed by Scandinavian artists. Much of their
music recalls the ancient bards and mythology. We are
taken back into primeval forests to hear the roar of Pan
and his companions; melodies descend from mountain
peaks and echo from icy streams and rivers.

Among the most striking examples of nature music from
Scandinavia are these pieces:

Jan Sibelius (Finland) - The Bard (EMI - ASD 3340)
En Saga (London 6745)
Swan of Tuonela (Columbia M-34548)
Karelia Overture (RCA ARL-2613)
Tapiola (Seraphim 60000)
The seven Symphonies (miscellaneous labels). Deva
music of power.
Sibelius's music brings forth awesome Nature forces.

Edvard Grieg (Norway) - Lyric Suite (Melodiya
   Angel S-40048)
Piano Concerto (RCA ARL-3059)
Peer Gynt (London STS-15040)
String music (BIS-LP-147)
Miscellaneous songs and piano music
Grieg gives us the music of Nature's little folk, such as the
fairies.

Carl Nielsen (Denmark) - The Dream of Gunnar; Pan
   and Syrinx; Rhapsodie Overture (Seraphim
   SIC-6098, 3 records)
The six Symphonies (various labels)

Franz Berwald (Sweden) - Symphonies (various
   labels)
Memories of Norwegian Alps, and others
   (Seraphim S-6113)

Rued Langgaard (Denmark) - Symphony No. 4
(Defoliage) (EMI-063 38100)

Lars-Erik Larsson (Sweden) - Pastoral Suite (Swedish
Society SLT 33 176)

Christian Sinding (Norway) - Piano Concerto (Candide 31110)

RUSSIAN AND SLAVIC

Again, much of this music pictures ancient legends and
fairy tales, some colorful and enchanting (Tchaikovsky
and Rimsky-Korsakov), while other is of a devic quality,
lovely, but unearthly and remote (Scriabin and, to a lesser
degree, Liadov).

Antonin Dvořák (Czech)
In Nature's Realm (DGG 2530785)
The Silent Woods (Philips Festivo 6570112)
Symphony No. 8 (Odyssey 33231)
Symphony No. 9 ("From the New World") (London
   21025)
Cello Concerto (DGG 2535106)

Dvořák's music is filled with the beauty of nature. Dvořák was essentially a lyricist, combining Slavic melodies—often in a Brahmsian way—with the songs of the American Indian and the Negro spirituals, these last, more in Dvořák's later works.

Peter Tchaikovsky (Russian) - Swan Lake and Sleeping Beauty (various labels)
Symphony No. 1 (Winter Dreams) (DGG 2530078)

Alexander Scriabin (Russian) - Poem of Fire (London 6732)
Poem of Ecstasy (DGG 2530137)
Late piano sonatas (music of nature devas)

Anatol Liadov (Russian) - The Enchanted Lake, Baba-Yaga (London STS-15066)

Bedrich Smetana (Czech) - The Moldau River and The High Castle (2 Turnabout 34619 / 20)

Rimsky-Korsakov (Russian) - Sadko (London CS-6036)
Golden Cockerel (Melodiya Angel S-40259)

See the Appendix for additional selections of nature music and music of the four seasons.

7

cAn&elic cMusic

> ...the choir invisible, whose music is the
> gladness of the world.
>
> F. Delius

Spiritual teachings inform us to "Go to God first, and to others as God directs." We are attended by those who are more highly evolved than we at this stage of our development. Such a group of helpers open to us are the angels. These radiant Hosts of God are mentioned approximately three hundred times in the Bible, and they are also exalted in other world religions and contemporary spiritual writings, such as Geoffrey Hodson's *The Brotherhood of Angels and Men*. Flower A. Newhouse, spiritual teacher and clairvoyant Christian mystic, has written with illumination and insight into the Kingdom of the Angels. Her books *Rediscovering the Angels* and *The Kingdom of the Shining Ones* are classics in their field and offer us much information into the ways of angels. The Reverend Newhouse says in *Kingdom of the Shining Ones* (p. 19):

> There are four great waves of Angelic life attuned primarily to physical existence and to serving that life which is active within the planet. There are many other great Angelic paths—all of them purposeful and glorious—but they do not concern us. One of these four paths is that of

the "Nature Wave." The second is called the "Life Motivation Wave." The third is associated with the releasement of Divine Wisdom's expression. The fourth is known as the "Wave of Love."

She explains how these great beings of Light bless mankind with many different, empowering activities. Among these waves of Angelic life are God's legions who bless nature and the elements, heightening their beauty, graceful forms and colors.

Other angels help to direct God's healing Light. These great ones focus renewing energies into hospitals, homes, places of work, churches, schools and all areas that are receptive and needy. Other messengers inspire mankind through the beauty and joy of the creative arts.

There are joy-filled harmonies and melodious sounds which the angels help to focus into our atmosphere, and we will hear this music of the spheres as we can become more centered and attuned in Light. Watcher angels and guardian angels remain near us, encouraging us to live finer lives, which are more dedicated to Truth and loving unselfish service. Great warrior angels combat evil with power.

Our consciousness is not limited to time. At any moment, "through inspiration or desperation," we can come into attunement with Light, which enables us to receive inpourings in many forms from higher sources. So it is with many of the great composers. In the midst of many good works, they seem to have had those moments when they were especially inspired. During these moments, Light poured through them, and angelic harmonies filled their being and atmosphere. Some composers, like Handel during his writing of *Messiah*, even saw the Angelic Hosts and gave them full credit for whatever inspiration they were able to transmit into notes and melodies.

Today we have a few musical compositions which seem angelically inspired. These special pieces seem to bless

those listeners who hear them, and they bring angelic
vibrations into any atmosphere where they are played.
Angelic music brings Light. It is usually joyful, piercingly
clear and bright. Often, such music echoes the singing of
celestial choirs contained in bell-like and harp-like sounds.
Certain of these pieces of music also bring in strong healing
energies and are especially beneficial when played in
hospitals, nursing homes, or in rooms with mentally
disturbed patients. Other angelic music, such as Wagner's
"Ride of the Valkyries," brings strength, while music like
Gluck's "Dance of the Blessed Spirits" brings in the quality
of joy.

In all of the following pieces of music, angelic presences
can be felt by those who are sensitive to them. This music
opens doorways into the angelic atmosphere of Light.
Listen to these pieces repeatedly, for they are filled with
heavenly echoes which can purify and heighten your life.

Grieg - Nocturne (from Lyric Suite)
This music brings into the atmosphere an angel of the
night, who blesses nature and life forms.

Gluck - Dance of the Blessed Spirits
Music that emanates energies of joy and renewal.

Beethoven - Piano Concerto No. 5 (Emperor), second
movement
The quiet transparency of this music is one of Beethoven's
most beautiful and haunting achievements.

Mozart - Laudate Dominum, Psalm 116, (from
Vesperae Solennes de Confessore)
Piano Concerto No. 21 (slow movement)
Both pieces raise the listener into celestial realms.

Brahms - Piano Concerto No. 2, 3d movement
The melodies in the cello and piano bring openings into the
angelic realms.

Berlioz - Hosanna (from L'Enfance du Christ)
Sanctus (from Requiem)
The choral singing here is light and transparent, lifting the
listener upward in consciousness into angelic ethers.

Humperdinck - Children's Prayer (from Hansel and Gretel)
This beautiful music, leading into high strings, always brings angelic Presences into the atmosphere.

Vaughan Williams - Fantasia on a Theme of Thomas Tallis
The soaring strings echo Angelic harmonies.
Shepherds of the Delectable Mountains (from Pilgrim's Progress)
The chorus of Angels welcomes the Pilgrim into celestial regions, upon his transition from earth life.

Franck - Panis Angelicus (Pavarotti)
Franck, himself, is said to be from the angelic kingdom, and much of his music channels this essence.

Mahler - Symphony No. 2 (Resurrection)
The rising finale reaches into the celestial realms—chorus and orchestra soar into the angelic.
Symphony No. 8
This great work, demanding 1000 players, is a cosmic vision, lifting the listener into great Light.

Handel - Hallelujah Chorus (from Messiah)
Probably the greatest angel music ever composed. Handel saw angels descending and filling his room as he received their inspired thought forms while composing this part of Messiah.

Bohm - Calm as the Night (for organ)
A quiet, meditative, yet very powerful piece of music, suggesting the eternal serenity of the heavens.

Chopin - Nocturne in E-flat (Op. 9. No. 2)
Piano Concerto No. 1 (slow movement)
Andante Spianato
All these pieces open up angelic tones and harmonies.

Wagner - Ride of the Valkyries
Strong sounds of empowering warrior angels cleanse the atmosphere and call the listener to take courage.
Prelude to Parsifal

The music of Holy Grail, lifting the listener into Hosts and shining presences.

Prelude (Act I) to Lohengrin

Wagner actually saw angels descending and rising in the golden radiance of the Grail theme.

Evening Star (Tannhauser)

Bruckner - Symphony No. 8 (Adagio)

This is music of the night, suggesting forests and high mountain peaks. It is Bruckner's painting of the Archangel Michael, combating evil forces.

Respighi - Pines of Rome, 3d movement

This section of the work suggests the nature devas and angelic presences.

Paul Horn - Inside the Taj Mahal

The flute tones, soaring upward in the ambient, transparent acoustics of the marvelous Taj Mahal, link the listener with angelic harmonies.

Mendelssohn - How Lovely Are Thy Messengers and Sanctus (from Elijah)

The reverence and devotion of Mendelssohn's sacred music here raise the listener into angelic contact.

J. S. Bach - Sanctus (from B-minor Mass)

Powerful music; soaring celestial choirs make connection with angelic forces.

Rubinstein - Angelic Dream (from Kamennoi Ostrov)

Magical music, moving one into angelic realms with beautiful, suggestive themes.

Schubert - Ave Maria

The rising, devotional quality of the music makes angelic forces come near.

Bach-Gounod - Ave Maria

Also very beautiful, devotional music.

Gounod - Sanctus (from Misse Solenelle)

This is a very ceremonial kind of Angelic music, which welcomes the angels into the atmosphere—very powerful.

Thomé - Andante Religioso
Contains the theme of the Holy Spirit.

Hammerstein - Climb Every Mountain (from Sound of Music)
This music seems to contain the sounding of one's guardian angel to do better and to achieve necessary overcomings in our lifetime. It brings in the tone and power of great courage.

Prologue (from Sound of Music)
Calls of angelic and deva presences, echoing to each other from great Alpine peaks.

Pachelbel - Canon in D

Braga - Angel's Serenade

Casals - Song of the Birds

Marx-Gerda - Guardian Angels (sung by Mario Lanza)

Elgar - Pomp and Circumstance, No. 1

Rodrick White - Bright Messenger

These hymns, from various denominations and traditions, contain angelic tunes and also words that praise these great Hosts with joy and devotion:

Hymns:

O Holy Night (by Adam)
Ye Watchers and Ye Holy Ones (tune: Lasst Uns Erfreuen)
Ye Holy Angels Bright (tune: Darwall's 148th)
Angels from the Realms of Glory (tune: Regent Square, Henry T. Smart)
Angels We Have Heard on High (tune: Gloria)
(These hymns can be found in the Congregational Hymnal, United Church of Christ.)

You can never go wrong playing these pieces of great music. Such angelic music is always highly therapeutic, inspirational and spiritually elevating. It brings noticeable empowerment and clears the aura.

Let the bright Seraphim in burning row,
Their loud uplifted Angel-trumpets blow;
Let the Cherubic Host, in tuneful choirs
Touch their immortal harps with golden wires;
Let their celestial concerts all unite,
Ever to sound His praise in endless morn
of Light.

Samson by Handel

8

Music to God and The Christ

> *It is the whole of my being, Lord Christ, that you*
> *would have me give you, tree and fruit alike,*
> *the finished work as well as the harnessed*
> *power, the OPUS together with the operation.*
> Teilhard de Chardin

A close look at the great composers' lives and music shows
how often a higher inspiration accompanied and inspired
their efforts. Most of the composers who acknowledged
this Presence, which worked with them and through them,
were outside particular religious institutions or affiliations.
Yet, as we examine the great composers' diaries and letters,
we find that they openly named the Presence according to
their own experience of direct communion and contact. In
many instances the composers have called this Presence
God or Christ, realizing that such inspirations are cosmic
sources of power, which are both transcendent yet extremely close and intimate in their lives. Regardless of any
particular religion or philosophy held by these artists,
whenever they were open and receptive, the divine
radiance came upon them, illumining their creativity like a
golden fire. In these instances the composer becomes the
connective channel which transmits closer communion
between mankind and the Creater God. As Corinne Heline
puts it: "The highest mission of music is to serve as a link

between God and men. It builds a bridge over which angelic hosts can come closer to mankind."

If we look at the personalities of great composers, we often find certain unrefined weaknesses or challenges yet unbalanced in their character and temperament. But even in the midst of such shortcomings, higher impulses often outshine these imperfections. Even with all their human limitations—Wagner's racial prejudices, egocentricity and irresponsible behavior, Beethoven's temper tantrums and brusqueness, etc.—it seems that Divine Light invaded their human efforts, often lifting and transforming ordinary works into timeless masterpieces that stimulate mankind's evolution. Beethoven seemed aware of his human frailty as well as his divine gift when he said: "Divine One, Thou lookest into my inmost soul, thou knowest that love of man and desire to do good live therein... O God, give me strength to conquer myself; nothing must chain me to life."

After much research, I have found in the lives of the great composers many instances where their dedication to God was strong and overrode any particular religious affiliations. Mozart wrote in his journals: "I prayed to God, and the symphony began." J.S. Bach affirmed: "The aim and final reason for all music should be nothing else but the glory of God and the refreshment of the spirit." Beethoven, coming closer to God through much suffering, in his diary stated his final position of acceptance as a composer and a man, when he said: "I will humbly submit to all life's chances and changes, and put my sole trust in Thy immutable goodness, O God." The great Bohemian composer Antonin Dvořák always prefaced his scores with the words, "Thanks be to God," and the devotional Austrian master Anton Bruckner dedicated his Ninth Symphony "To Beloved God." The motto on many of Vivaldi's scores was "Glory to God and the blessed Mary."

Handel describes his ecstatic experience while writing the *Messiah*: "I did think I did see all Heaven before me—and the great God Himself. Whether I was in my body or out of my body as I wrote it, I know not. God knows." Haydn tells of his joy in the Lord: "God has given me a cheerful heart.... Whenever I think of the Dear Lord, I have to laugh. My heart jumps for joy in my breast." While composing *Parsifal*, Wagner set forth his spiritual credo: "I believe in God, Mozart, and Beethoven, and in their disciples and apostles; I believe in the Holy Spirit and the truth of art—one and indivisible; I believe that the art of music proceeds from God and dwells in the hearts of all enlightened men. ...I rejoice in one thought and consideration, the results of which might yet bring a great healing to the world...that I should be able to make clear Christ."

Although accused of being an agnostic, Ralph Vaughan Williams made the following proclamation: "Music is not a science only, but a divine voice. ...Divine Grace is dancing; dance ye therefore." Janáček, speaking about his *Slavonic Mass*, said: "I want to show people how to talk with God." Berlioz, writing to a friend about *L'Enfance du Christ*, said: "It seems to me to contain a feeling of the infinite, of divine love."

Franck, speaking to his friend and student D'Indy, said: "The joy of the world is transformed and flourishing by the Word of Christ." Speaking of his own faith, in his biography of Franck, D'Indy says, "The origin of music...is to be found incontestably in religion. The earliest song was a prayer. To praise God, to celebrate the beauty, the joy, and even the terrors of religion, was the sole object of all works of art for nearly 800 years." Arthur Abell in transcribing his conversation with his friend Brahms wrote: "Who else of all the countless millions of men who have trod this earth could compare with Christ? He taught righteousness, honesty in our dealings with our fellow men and He knew there is a life beyond the grave and that we earn it by faith and by keeping the commandments. Christ came as a great example to us, not as an exception." Also Brahms, regarded by some as a crusty agnostic, made this statement of faith to Arthur Abell: "I feel vibrations that thrill all of me. These are the Spirit illuminating the soul power within, and in this exalted state, I see clearly what is obscure in my ordinary moods. Then I feel capable of drawing inspiration from above, as Beethoven did. . . . I realize that I and my Father are one."

The composer Gustav Mahler was reared a Jew, but his longing for the Spirit was so strong that his deepest aspirations far exceeded any one faith or religion. We hear his devotion and heightened spiritual contact as they come through so strongly inspired in his own words which he wrote for the choral finale of his Symphony No. 2 (*Resurrection*):

> O all pervading pain,
> You I have escaped.
> O all-conquering death,
> Now you are conquered.
> With wings that I have won for myself
> In fervent loving aspiration
> Will I soar
> To the light that no eye has ever seen.
> I shall die, that I may live.
> Arise, yes. You will arise
> My heart, in a moment.
> What you have borne will carry you to God.

From these and many other recorded statements in journals and letters of the great composers, it is clear that when the Spirit has inspired the uplifted soul and the surrendered ego, and where talent has been cultivated sufficiently, great art can follow.

In music and our lives, we are emerging out of chaos into a new order. The cult of ugliness, glorification of the ego, and selfish, narrow provincialism are slowly moving into new horizons of beauty, self-giving and planetary cooperation. Today a new synthesis in the arts is emerging slowly, combining the best of the old with the new and unexpected. However, much of today's music seems transitional. Many styles of merely intellectually oriented music must undergo change.

There is also a spiritual renaissance on the horizon and a new hungering for the Divine, often coming about through necessity, not just choice. Some artists feel this development, slowly coming into view. George Rochberg, a contemporary American composer, who spent many years in serialism and atonal experiments, recently stated his new artistic credo: "The business of art is to praise God." And John Nelson, Music Director and Conductor of the Indianapolis Symphony Orchestra, recently shared his love of God and the Christ in these words:

> Some of the blocks (in a person) arise because of your own inadequacies, and others because of circumstances, and often I get these two confused. If I don't do my work well and then something doesn't go right, it's my fault, my frustration. Other times I have done my work well and I have been stopped. Both have been present in my life.
>
> I do believe as a Christian that if I do my work well and I follow what I know to be God's Will for me, then things are made rather clear, or—if they're not made clear—you know they're not clear for a reason, and you accept the situation.

Later on in the interview, reported in the *Christian Herald*, May 1979, Maestro Nelson talks about the difference between straight talent and creative gifts that he believes are inspired by the Christ Light:

> There is special joy in finding a singer who brings not only a beautiful instrument, his voice, to a part, but the inner Christian conviction. You can find soloists all over the place who will deliver the music beautifully and well, but there must be something deeper than that.

Irrespective of one's particular religious affiliation or credal acceptance, every person is *potentially* spiritual in his or her deepest makeup. Whatever his inclination or tradition, as he decides to draw upon this spiritual impulse and soul energy in praise and gratefulness, his life opens and the Divine Light enters his efforts. Many unexpected adventures then take him along new roads of travel in the Spirit. His life speeds forward, through increased testings, and the all-embracing Spirit and many unseen helpers of God heighten each moment of his day.

Certain pieces of music have been deeply inspired by a love of God and the Christ. Such music is spiritual in its deepest essence. It can raise our consciousness and spiritual attunement as we experience it.

Here is a list of musical selections, composed in the light of inspiration and devotion to God and the Living Christ:

Handel - Messiah
Wagner - Parsifal (Legend of the Holy Grail)
J.S. Bach - Jesu, Joy of Man's Desire
   Christmas Oratorio
   St. John Passion
   St. Matthew Passion
Berlioz - L'Enfance du Christ
Rheinberger - Star of Bethlehem
Mendelssohn - There Shall a Star from Jacob (from
   Christus)
   Elijah
Kaplan - Glorious (the Psalms)
Bloch - Sacred Service
Vivaldi - Gloria
Casals - The Manger
Ives - A Christmas Carol
Hovhaness - Magnificat
Britten - A Ceremony of Carols
Vaughan Williams - The Sons of Light
   Hodie (This Day)
   Fantasia on Christmas Carols

Virgil Fox - Christmas
   Great Protestant Hymns
Malotte - The Lord's Prayer
Elgar - The Light of Life
Parry - Ode on the Nativity
   Jerusalem
   I Was Glad
Fauré - Requiem
Mahler - Symphony No. 2 (Resurrection)
Mozart - Ave Verum Corpus
   Coronation Mass
   Exultate, Jubilate
Franck - Beatitudes
   Panis Angelicus
Brahms - A German Requiem
Rachmaninoff - Vespers
Liszt - Christus
Haydn, F.J. - The Creation
   Masses
Bruckner - Symphony No. 9
   Te Deum
Gounod - St. Cecilia Mass
R. Whiting - God Be With You Till We Meet Again
Fischer - Mass for Freedom
Zamfir - To You, O God
Cash - Gospel Road
Mario Lanza - I'll Walk With God
Nelhybel - Praise Ye the Lord
Palestrina - Pope Marcellus Mass
Monteverdi - Vespers of the Blessed Virgin (1610)
Byrd - Mass for Five Voices
Schubert - Ave Maria
Beethoven - Christ on the Mount of Olives
Enjoy Jesus - Hour of Power, Rev. Robert Schuller
Spirit Alive - Monks of the Weston Priory
      (Weston, Vermont)
Alfred Hill - Symphony (Joys of Life)

O my soul, for thee what remains now to do,
but to bend thy pride before such a mystery!
O my heart, fill now with a love deep and pure
That alone can guide us to a heavenly abode.
Berlioz, *L'Enfance du Christ*
Words of the invisible angelic chorus

Lord Christ, you who are as gentle as the
human heart, as fiery as the forces of nature, as
intimate as life itself, you in whom I can melt
away and with whom I must have mastery and
freedom: I love you as a world, as this world
which has captivated my heart. It is you, I now
realize, that my brother-men, even those who
do not believe, sense and seek throughout the
magic immensities of the cosmos.
Pierre Teilhard de Chardin

9

cA Gallery of Great Composers

> *We composers are projectors of the infinite into the finite.*
>
> Grieg

Each composer, as a channel for great music, brings through a particular keynote. From the music of each great artist you will receive a particular quality of energy that sounds through you. Such energy, transmitted through great masterpieces of music, will affect each person both specifically and generally. You can learn how to use certain pieces of music to rebalance yourself and help you meet definite needs and challenges in life. Certain musical selections are like tuning forks which will empower and center you to life's harmony.

While some of your tastes might change through the years, other tendencies will become even stronger with time. With the help of your deepest desires, temperament, and momentum from many choices in the past, you will find those musical works that speak most directly to you.

Learn to keep a list of the musical selections that help you the most. Observe how they affect you and when they are most timely. Like very close friends, such pieces of music will always sustain and nourish you, and you can return to them with trust and confidence. Expand your acquaintance with great music, so that you can make new contacts. Explore new composers and new compositions, and be alert, ready to sense the music that is most beautiful and therapeutic for you. Stay away from composers and music that do nothing for you.

The greatness of music as a healing agent in your life lies in its continuous becoming. Music never stands still; it is always new and forever alive, bringing in fresh potencies of melody, rhythm and harmonizing energies that fill you. Use musical selections like large, healing fountains. Feel their liquid streams of sound pouring through you. Let your music bathe and cleanse you.

As I now introduce the following great composers and their music, I mean for my descriptions to be suggestive, not literal. For each great artist and his music, I have tried to share personal impressions, feelings and inner responses. You may hear entirely different qualities in a piece of music or even a composer's total output. This is good. My hope is that your love for this music will increase and that my comments may only be springboards to help you find the music most inspiring to you that will bring clearance and new openings into Light.

GREGORIAN CHANTS AND EARLIER MUSIC

I recommend to you the very beautiful and exalted music of Gregorian Chant. Often such music is sung by monks or nuns who live the monastic life. Because of the original, spiritual motivation that is contained in Gregorian chants, you will often feel a reverence, deeper devotion and a privacy that is removed from earthly stress and turmoil. Gregorian music is not sensational; it does not contain many sudden changes or shifts in tempo. It connects you with the Eternal, and it awakens true humility and devotion. These chants are a good way to defuse after a stressful day, for their celestial resonance can lift you out of the mundane. This music also contains a spaciousness which awakens adoration and opens you to hear the echoes of the heavens singing. Gregorian music is restful, strengthening and clearing to the system. It is something you can "disappear into," another world of peace and flow that is a powerful antidote to the tensions and uncertainties of our times. Without listening to this music as an escapist, you can find much in it that is constructive and empowering.

I remember experiencing an unforgettable moment while listening to some Gregorian chants in Cambridge, England, some years ago. It was evening, and there was a peacefulness in the air, and the sun shone through the stained glass windows of the chapel at King's College. Suddenly, a small group of robed choristers began to walk down the aisle of the chapel, as though they were fulfilling an ancient ritual. The young boys began to sing Gregorian chants, which included some Psalms. I remember the powerful sense of Presence I experienced as the music made me feel transparent and filled with Light. The music lifted me in consciousness, and a timeless space and peace surrounded me. I remember the power of this experience, and shortly afterwards, tried to suggest what I had felt, as I wrote these lines:

> This evening boys are singing
> anthems ancient as their chapel home,
> A canticle of golden pure soprano song
> from holiness so young
> thrills and shivers the stained glass.
> The youthful choristers sing praises
> while sound is playing on their faces
> and shaping Light forever from the One.
>
> From the plexus of the solar fires,
> music calls its kingly choirs.
> All the chanters of the sounding hours,
> hearing echoes through the heart and bone
> create the marrow of all singing,

become translucent,
resounding Divinity alone.

When you wish to experience peace and the timeless grandeur of the Divine Presence, listen to these selections of Gregorian music and early polyphonic compositions:

Pope Marcellus Mass
Chants from Assisi
Midnight Mass for Christmastide
Benedictine Nuns
Gregorian Anthology
Feast of Michaelmas
Trappist Monks' Choir
Come to the Quiet—Beautiful, contemporary
    music of devotion—in monastic tradition.

Below are sketches of some of the greatest composers. I have included alongside each one the element (Fire, Earth, Air, Water) which seems to be strongest in the music he composes. Of course, all these energies are to some degree present, but usually one or two are dominant in the music of each. I have also listed the astrological sign for each composer, for their signs are related to the elements, as explained in Chapter 3.

ANTONIO VIVALDI
(Pisces—Water)

I like Vivaldi's beautiful melodies—effervescent, flowing like a stream. His music is usually happy, uncomplicated, warm and genial. At times you can hear imitations of nature songs and bird calls. In my work as a music therapist, I have found that Vivaldi's bright music is good for emotional and mental clearance. It does not intrude and is always good company. In some nursing homes and other environments where I have worked, Vivaldi's music has seemed to clear the atmosphere with its vitality and rhythmical clarity. At home, the concertos for flute and piccolo are good company during meals, and they aid digestion. You can write letters to a friend to the background of Vivaldi.

Main works: The Four Seasons; Mandolin Concertos; Flute Concertos; Gloria; Credo; Piccolo Concertos; Sacred Choral Works

I especially recommend an album of Vivaldi's music, Koto Flute (Angel S-3732S), which offers four Vivaldi concertos, played with a flute and accompanied by a Koto orchestra. The textures are clear and beautiful.

GEORG PHILIPP TELEMANN
(Pisces—Water)

I find much in Telemann's music that is similar to the qualities of Vivaldi's music. Again, there is vitality and the melodies are clear. There is a sense of freedom and flow. Telemann's music is gentle, yet ordered and strong.

You can plan your day to the background of a Telemann concerto. His music is good for clearing the mind while driving to work in the morning. Its melodies are cheerful and relieve stress. Telemann's music gets you through traffic on the highway. It is also an intimate friend into the night.

Main works: Music for the Banquet Table; Suite for Flute and Strings; Water Music; miscellaneous concertos

GEORGE FRIDERIC HANDEL
(Aquarius-Pisces—Air-Water)

I like the feelings of majesty and nobility that I hear in Handel's music. His finest music contains strong feeling and ordered action-movement. It is often formal, traditional and conventional. Boundaries are never broken, yet within the containment there is soaring and elevation of the spirit. Handel's music is also ceremonial, serious, at times ornate. There is usually greater celestial joy than human merriment. He is more concerned with raising human consciousness to view divine vistas than in probing into human conditions. Handel's music is stirring.

I believe that the greatest music Handel ever composed is *Messiah*, especially the "Hallelujah Chorus." As this music poured into his room, he reports that he was so inspired and "on fire" that he could hardly keep his pen moving fast enough to represent what he was hearing. During these moments Handel reports seeing the Heavenly Host, who filled him with these Christ-lighted sounds. He felt this music was truly not his own, and for this reason, in reverence, he never charged for a single performance of *Messiah*. All proceeds were given to charity. Those who are sensitive feel that even now this music brings in the angels.

Main works: Messiah; Harp Concertos; Organ Concertos; Water Music; Ode to Saint Cecilia; Royal Fireworks Music; Judas Maccabaeus

JOHANN SEBASTIAN BACH
(Pisces-Aries—Water-Fire)

To me Bach's music brings through the power and grandeur of God. His music is universal and echoes the immensity of the heavens moving in their orbits. His textures are thickly orchestrated, yet even solo instruments sound exactly appropriate.

Bach's music is both masculine and feminine. Reason and emotion are blended with total sureness and solidity. I feel that Bach's music is the unfailing statement that Light conquers darkness and Good will overcome evil. At its best, his music echoes the celestial choirs whose music fills the earth. The choruses from his cantatas are most inspiring; a listener cannot help but be lifted out of depression and stagnation. Bach's music is contained, yet vast.

Bach composed all his music in worship and with a desire "to glorify God." This music can change people's lives and brings new openings. I remember how the power and joy of the Third Brandenburg Concerto helped a friend find courage to save his marriage. Listen to Bach's music to clear and activate your mind.

Main works: Toccata and Fugue in D; B-minor Mass; Saint Matthew Passion; Saint John Passion; Brandenburg Concertos; Magnificat; Christmas Oratorio; Suites for Orchestra; Jesu Joy of Man's Desiring

CHRISTOPH WILLIBALD GLUCK
(Cancer—Water)

I like the simplicity and naturalness of Gluck's music. It is always in good taste and unifies feelings with ideas of form.

A piece of beautiful music that is always cleansing is the joyful "Dance of the Blessed Spirits." This ten-to-twelve-minute piece of music seems to clear the air, and it brings a purifying uplift to the listener. It is celestial music.

Main works: Concerto in G for Flute; Don Juan; Orfeo and Euridice

FRANZ JOSEPH HAYDN
(Aries—Fire)

Haydn's music is sharp and fresh; it sparkles with zestful tunes and rhythms. Haydn, himself, says that as he composed his music he heard it crackle like notes flying from a spindle. His music is optimistic, joyful, clean and always in good spirit. It has good energy—it effervesces. It is said that Haydn in joy and gratitude always dressed in his finest garments and wore his costliest wig when he sat down to compose, for he felt that when he was in the presence of music, he was also in the Presence of the Creator.

Play Haydn's music to disperse depression or gloom. Haydn will help you to see and feel the bright side. His music is like bright diamonds of energy that will shimmer through rigid attitudes or negative emotions. His choral music is often worshipful and luminous with joy. Haydn's music empowers the listener.

Main works: The Seasons; The Creation; the Symphonies; Quartets; Organ Concertos; Masses; Trumpet Concerto

WOLFGANG AMADEUS MOZART
(Aquarius—Air)

I find Mozart's music uniquely different in quality and essence from other composers'. It is somewhat elusive, mysterious, at times will-o-the-wisp, and even angelic. It is always refined, elegant and charming.

For me, it is the airy, unrestricted quality of Mozart's music that is so beautiful. Working within the musical form and period of his times, he somehow transcended it and achieved a transparent joy.

His use of the orchestra brings through music that is crystalline in its clarity. Yet Mozart's music is also powerful and radiant. A certain poignancy in some works reveals a human being who suffered greatly but never indulged himself for long in moodiness. To me a devotional quality pervades his music, along with the airy lightness. Mozart's music belongs to a world all its own.

Main works: Magic Flute; piano concertos; masses; string quartets; string quintets; symphonies; violin concertos; serenades

LUDWIG VAN BEETHOVEN
(Sagittarius—Fire)

Beethoven's is the music of a titan. His life and works break open new entries into human emotions and the human condition. Beethoven is the first real musical psychologist, one who explores the psyche of mankind's sufferings and helps humanity to grow. This is music that throbs with joys and sorrows. Like vast primal energy, Beethoven's music unleashes great waves of power in the listener. Sometimes angry, sometimes peaceful, his music is full of the fighting spirit, courage and strong will power, sometimes granite-like in its force. But it can also be tender and lyrical, devotional, sterling.

In my work with patients, I find that one piece of Beethoven's at a time is ample. Some of his symphonies (especially Nos. 3, 5, 6, 7 and 9) are like experiencing a complete lifetime of feeling and movement.

For many, Beethoven's music broadens relationships and awakens compassion and the desire for universal brotherhood. Because of the empathy contained in Beethoven's music, it stirs groups and crowds and lifts them to the point of human fulfillment and divine realization. Beethoven's music is like a royal warrior—robed in orange and purple.

Main works: the nine symphonies; Creatures of Prometheus; Missa Solemnis; piano concertos; Fidelio; Violin Concerto; the quartets

FRANZ SCHUBERT
(Aquarius—Air)

I like the private world of Schubert. His music reminds me of the wanderer in eternity, never at home on earth, yet warm and good-hearted while passing through. Schubert's music is that of a loner among friends, living between love and pain, sensing peace behind life's transience.

Three of the most helpful pieces of Schubert's music for me are "Rosamunde," "Ave Maria" and the Symphony No. 8 (*Unfinished*). Persons that I work with respond very favorably to these selections, finding in them a reassurance, calm power and deep, inward awakenings. The "Ave Maria" is music of unconditional love, devotion and surrender that transmutes sorrow.

Main works: Ave Maria; the nine symphonies; masses; string quartets; songs; piano works; Rosamunde

FELIX MENDELSSOHN
(Aquarius—Air)

Whereas Beethoven stirs up, Mendelssohn soothes with serenity. His music contains an aristocratic refinement and an ennobling joy. I often sense beautiful landscapes, painted in shades of green and turquoise, as I experience Mendelssohn's music.

I find it good for calming tense and agitated patients. The Symphony No. 4 (*Italian*) and the overtures "Calm Sea and Prosperous Voyage" and "The Hebrides" bring in healing energies that cleanse the atmosphere. Mendelssohn's music also revives the sick and lonely, and it relieves tiredness.

Main works: A Midsummer Night's Dream; the symphonies; Violin Concerto; Elijah; St. Paul; Calm Sea and Prosperous Voyage; On Wings of Song; Songs Without Words

FREDERIC CHOPIN
(Pisces—Water)

Like Mendelssohn's music, Chopin's works are always refined. But instead of painting outer landscapes, Chopin's music portrays soulscapes of feeling. A deep emotional content fills his piano works. I also hear nobility, some nostalgia and romance in Chopin's finest works. His music is like water, ever shifting in its contours, shadings and colors. Sometimes a quiet stream, again a torrent, his music is forever fluid, carrying the listener through an ever-changing flow of human emotions.

I feel the essence of Chopin to be contained in these words about him from his contemporaries:

A man of exquisite heart and mind.

Delacroix

His soul was a star and dwelt apart.

. . . .

He was a lover of an Impossible so shadowy and so near the stellar regions.

George Sand

What others say on their knees, he uttered in tone-language—all the mysteries of passion and grief which man can understand without words, because there are no words in which they can adequately be expressed.

Franz Liszt

I have found that Chopin's music strikes deeply into human loneliness. Several introverts with whom I have worked responded favorably to Chopin's Waltzes; Nocturne, Op. 9, No. 2; and the Piano Concerto No. 1 (slow movement).

Main works: Etudes; preludes; impromptus; waltzes; nocturnes; ballades; the two piano concertos; scherzos; polonaises; mazurkas; Andante Spianato

ROBERT SCHUMANN
(Gemini—Air)

It is the childlike quality of Schumann's music that I respond to the most. I also like his ability to capture in music the essence of thought and ideas. His music reworks literary scenes and themes, transforming them into musical melodies and interior landscapes. Schumann's music combines the language of the head and the heart.

Most helpful to me in my own life and work have been these works: "Traumerei" ("Dreams"), Symphony No. 1 (*Spring*), "Childhood Scenes," and the Piano Concerto.

Main works: The four symphonies; Manfred; Scenes from Faust; quartets; Piano Concerto; Cello Concerto; miscellaneous piano works

JOHANNES BRAHMS
(Taurus—Earth)

Brahms' music combines a private, tender and loving heart with a feisty and rustic personality. You can hear the working out of inner conflict and great soul strength as you listen to Brahms. There is a toughness of fiber, thick sounds of orchestral melody, which seem to me to emerge out of deep forests and underbrush. Always a path leads into Light and clearance. There is deep love in the heart, never worn on the sleeve, and a powerful intellect that lives in company with peasant habits and scraggy beard.

A work like Brahms' Symphony No. 4 is solid, dependable and helps to ground you if you are feeling disconnected. The earthy power in his music helps to build a stronger foundation in your schedule and desires. Brahms' compositions are also filled with good humor and devotion (example, *Academic Festival* Overture).

Brahms' music also imparts an attunement with nature (especially in the Symphony No. 2), a hint of sadness, but never for more than an instant.

My favorite Brahms includes these pieces: "Lullaby"; Symphonies Nos. 1, 2, 3; piano concertos.

Main works: The four symphonies; Violin Concerto; A German Requiem; the two piano concertos; miscellaneous chamber music; songs

RICHARD WAGNER
(Taurus-Gemini—Earth-Air)

The key to appreciating Wagner's works is to realize that they contain human and superhuman energies. At times there seems to be an almost egomaniacal concern for self-power, and in other instances a clear channeling for divine power to inspire the music.

Reports from his contemporaries tell us that Wagner the man was unattractive, without scruples, totally self-centered, feeling that the world owed him a living. But as a composer Wagner remained totally loyal, single-minded and open to inspiration from higher powers in nature and the angelic Hosts.

Wagner's music is very powerful—filled with surging energies and bolts of electric currents. The best of Wagner's music stirs us to our depths. It brings spiritual contact, cosmic awareness and feelings of invincibility within the soul. However, too much of his music at one time can be exhausting.

You can use some of Wagner's works to ennoble and inspire your life. It can also make people become overbearing and power-hungry, even to the point of insanity and dementedness. Hitler listened to Wagner and worked himself up to the point of frenzy before going out to address his troops. Wagner's music is capable of bringing out the very best or the very worst.

The Wagnerian music that I have found to be most uplifting and inspiring includes these works: "Ride of the Valkyries," mighty calls from great warrior angels; Prelude to *Lohengrin* (Act I), filled with power, exaltation, and angelic Hosts descending to earth; "Prelude" and "Good Friday Spell" from *Parsifal*.

Main works: The Ring Cycle; Parsifal; Meistersinger; Lohengrin; Tristan and Isolde; Flying Dutchman; Siegfried Idyll (especially orchestral selections from these works)

CÉSAR FRANCK
(Sagittarius—Fire)

To me Franck's music is contemplative, filled with feelings of intimate devotion to God. It is largely empty of personal ego and channels into the atmosphere the harmonies of devas and angelic choirs. Franck's music can help us to become more receptive to presences beyond ourselves. It frees us to larger possiblities in the spirit. It is also filled with the powerful simplicity of true love. To me Franck's music is the sound of a world transformed by the Divine Presence—warm, spacious, privately enthroned. As Vincent D'Indy, Franck's student, said, "Franck's music is music of the center of the soul."

His music puts us at ease because it demands nothing from a listener. It pours forth its song, not always familiar, but strangely beautiful, other-worldly—like rarified air. Franck's music, that of the contemplative mystic, inspired me to write these lines:

> Listen to the sounds of great cathedrals
> steepling the heavens;
> hear the praising panoply of Angels
> filling earth.

Main works: Miscellaneous organ works; Symphony in D-minor; Piano Quintet in F; Symphonic Variations for Piano and Orchestra; the Beatitudes; Mass; Panis Angelicus (sung by Pavarotti)

MAX BRUCH
(Capricorn—Earth)

Bruch's music brings in a strong quality of heart and mind. His music seems grounded in the soil of human friendship, kindness and a warm love-nature. You can sing his melodies; and his violin works, especially, are always appealing and genial.

Bruch's music nourishes us and kindles devotion. It is reassuring more than stimulating.

Main works: The three violin concertos; Scottish Fantasy; Kol Nidrei; Serenade; In Memoriam; Concerto for two Pianos and Orchestra; Adagio

ANTONIN DVOŘÁK
(Virgo—Earth)

Dvořák's music is also earth music that brings joy and warmth. His music contains many beautiful melodies drawn from his native Bohemia, the songs of the American Indian, and Negro spirituals. I find also a strong presence of nature and feelings of love for humanity and friends. To me much of Dvořák's music surges with spiritual joy, affirmation and the grounded simplicity of the home and the good earth.

Dvořák's music has helped me in two specific counseling situations. I once tutored a young student who was at the time quite tense and troubled. The "Largo" from the 9th Symphony helped him to relax and to concentrate. In another instance I can remember how much happier a woman was after just listening quietly to "Humoresque."

One of the first musical favorites my wife and I shared together was the Cello Concerto, which both of us loved before we had ever met each other. Its melodies are beautiful, triumphant and filled with the lyrical songs of the heart.

Main works: The nine symphonies, especially Nos. 8 and 9 (From the New World); Cello Concerto; Humoresque; Slavonic Dances; Piano Concerto

EDVARD GRIEG
(Gemini—Air)

I always think of the "little beings" of nature—elves, gnomes, fairies, and so forth, and the music of great waterfalls and fjords of the North, as I listen to Grieg's music. I find it filled with enchanting, lyrical cameos of smaller nature presences. There is a Nordic freshness and open-air quality that purifies atmospheres wherever it is played. A joy and vitality also fill his music. It is enlivening.

Pay special attention to Grieg's "Nocturne" (from *Lyric Suite*) and the slow movement of the Piano Concerto. These selections seem to especially bring in healing radiations.

Though it is powerful music, it usually does not sound as awesome as Wagner's or Sibelius's landscapes. One of his most dramatic works is his Piano Concerto. Like Mendelssohn and Chopin before him, Grieg composed intimate tone portraits and vignettes of beauty. I find Grieg's music to be very therapeutic and well received by persons I counsel.

Main works: Piano Concerto; Holberg Suite; Peer Gynt; Olav Trygvason; I Love Thee (song); miscellaneous piano works; Lyric Suite; Two Elegiac Melodies; Norwegian Dances

PETER ILYICH TCHAIKOVSKY
(Taurus—Earth)

Tchaikovsky's music evokes inward dreams and reveries. There is a wistfulness to his music, which often stirs memories of fairy tales and magical realms. Along with this quality, Tchaikovsky's music also contains Slavic power, drama, occasional tints of melancholy and the Russian penchant for exploring the dark side of life.

I feel an attunement with nature in some of Tchaikovsky's music, especially Symphony No. 1, *Sleeping Beauty*, and occasionally in *Swan Lake*. A strong militant quality also is audible in the martial sections of "Marche slave," Symphony No. 5, and Symphony No. 6 (*Pathetique*). This music can empower you.

Be careful what selections of Tchaikovsky's music you play, for his works contain a wide range of emotional content. Find those selections which are inspiring to you, and do not play too often any pieces that cause you to remain in low moods or fantasies. I find that good energy raisers include Piano Concerto No. 1, Violin Concerto, Serenade for Strings, "Manfred," "Capriccio Italien," and selections from *The Nutcracker*.

Main works: The three piano concertos; the six symphonies; Manfred; Violin Concerto; Sleeping Beauty; Swan Lake; Nutcracker; Serenade for Strings;

Marche slave; Capriccio Italien; Variations on a Rococco Theme

FREDERICK DELIUS
(Aquarius—Air)

Delius's music is filled with the atmosphere of nature. The listener often feels an absence of human presence. In this sense it is removed, non-tactile, yet very real to the listener, who is taken inside nature's flowing rhythms, rather than remaining just an onlooker. This music is like an elusive breeze, bringing fragrance and passing by quickly. The winsomeness reminds us of the evanescent quality of life, the mingling relationships on earth, and the changing seasons of nature. It is universal music, belonging both everywhere and nowhere.

Delius's music requires time and attention. Some of my friends have said to me at first, "Nothing's happening! What's Delius saying?" Then, gradually, as they give themselves to the music, they will enter Delius's world. A special favorite among persons who hear Delius's music is "On Hearing the First Cuckoo in Spring." I find that his works (especially *Appalachia* and *Florida Suite*) are excellent for stirring the creative imagination. I remember with pleasure finger-painting to the sounds and harmonies of "Brigg Fair" and "Over the Hills and Far Away." The music produced a freeing effect on me.

Main works: Appalachia; Song of Summer; Florida Suite; Cello Concerto; A Mass of Life; On Hearing the First Cuckoo in Spring; Over the Hills and Far Away; Brigg Fair; Piano Concerto; Song of the High Hills

GUSTAV MAHLER
(Cancer—Water)

Mahler's music spans the whole range of human emotion and aspiration of the soul. Torment is sometimes present, but at its best (Symphonies Nos. 2, 3, 8, 9) Mahler's music rises to peaks of joy, fulfillment, radiant love and divine connection. Many feel the presence of the celestial choirs in the finale of glory in the Symphony No. 2 (*Resurrection*) and the surrender of the soul in the expansive Adagio of the Symphony No. 9.

I hear assertiveness and power mingling with devotion and surrender as I experience Mahler's great symphonies and songs. There is a bitter-sweet quality that pervades Mahler's world. Suffering brings liberation. Resignation leads to release.

Mahler's works are composed for a very large symphony orchestra, so be prepared for a real bombardment in your atmosphere. His 8th Symphony is composed for more than one thousand performers, and it brings through a cosmic potency which Mahler reports that he clearly felt and envisioned. But along with power, love and devotion fill his music, and the 9th Symphony moves into final peace and illumination.

Main works: The ten symphonies; Song of the Earth; Songs of a Wayfarer

ANTON BRUCKNER
(Virgo—Earth)

Anton Bruckner devoted all his music to God Almighty. To me his music is cosmic, the great outpouring of a devotional Christian mystic. Layer by layer and stone by stone, each unfolding melody can lift you up toward mountain heights that reach into kingdoms of holy Light. His music always unfolds gradually, and often Bruckner likes to repeat his great themes, each time slightly differently, weaving an ascending spiral, opening on high until the whole sonic spiral is spread out. In many of Bruckner's symphonies and choral works there is a confrontation with evil, as clarion trumpets of Light come into darkness to fill it. Many of his symphonies last more than an hour, leading toward great heights.

Bruckner's scherzos are often spiced with nature beings and folk-like dances. These contrast with the more powerful sections. His finales ascend with peace and drama, lifting us higher and higher; they seem to leave us suspended in the company of the Infinite with great legions of heavenly beings. Though sometimes dark and nocturnal, Bruckner's music always eventually emerges into Light.

> Bruckner is one of those rare geniuses whose natural fate it was to make the supernatural real, to force the Divine into the straitjacket of our human world.
> Wilhelm Furtwangler

Listen to the sounds of harps in Bruckner's symphonies, especially in the adagio of the 8th Symphony. These sounds, like the glissandos of waterfalls in the night, represent angelic presences in our lives.

Main works: The nine symphonies; Te Deum, Psalm 150; motets; masses; String Quintet

ACHILLE CLAUDE DEBUSSY
(Leo-Virgo—Fire-Earth)

Debussy's music is music of the Water Kingdom, filled with glimpses into aqua worlds of nature, containing such beings as sylphs, naiads, sirens and undines from the deep.

I like the exotic quality and the pastoral feelings I experience in Debussy's works. The orchestration is precise; each instrument is like a voice which contributes to the very sensual colors and tones. Along with these, there is a peculiar healing quality in the music which frees the mind and breaks down rigidity.

Those pieces which have proved to be most beneficial to patients I have worked with include "Clair de lune" (awakening emotion and reverie), "The Sea" (dispersing mental tension and charging the listener), "Sacred and Profane Dances" for harp and orchestra, and "The Engulfed Cathedral" (awakening soul memories of distant kingdoms, rising out of oceans, then returning to complete submersion). "Images" energizes the listener with a color bath.

Main works: The Sea; Nocturnes; Images; Prelude to the Afternoon of a Faun; Sacred and Profane Dances; Clarinet Rhapsody; Clair de lune; Pelleas and Melisande

RALPH VAUGHAN WILLIAMS
(Libra—Air)

Here is nature music painting scenes in the English tradition, reminiscent of nature poems by Wordsworth and Arnold. It is the music of a spiritualized mind and a devotional heart. The music is sensitive to the human condition, while sensing the profound order in life. I feel the essential nobility in mankind as I listen to Vaughan Williams' works. The orchestral sound is powerful and robust. Yet there is calm attunement with nature ("Lark Ascending," Symphony No. 3) and compelling drama (Symphony No. 7 - *Antarctic*, composed for the cinema). "Lark Ascending" is a great favorite among most patients and friends.

Main works: Lark Ascending; Symphonies No. 1, 3, 5, 8; Fantasia on a Theme of Thomas Tallis; Fantasia on Greensleeves; Norfolk Rhapsody; A Pilgrim's Progress; Serenade to Music; In the Fen Country

I have tried to discuss as many of the greatest composers as I have room to include. To close this chapter, I want to share some impressions of some other artists and their works which I have found interesting and helpful.

FIRE COMPOSERS

These artists usually compose very powerful music, galvanic and highly energizing.

Modest Mussorgsky. His music extracts beauty from grossness and ugliness; it describes evil versus good, macabre versus serenity.

> Night on Bald Mountain; Boris Godunov

Bela Bartok. Bartok's music is often strange and impersonal; strange forces move in the night. In Bartok's pieces I feel music of a metallic mind and a heart trying to open. Bartok's shadow side surfaces in his music, chaotic and hard-driving; yet his personality was kind and quiet. I consider Bartok's music to be important as a historical stage of musical development, but I have not found it to be therapeutic or renewing.

> Concerto for Orchestra; Viola Concerto; Music for Strings, Percussion and Celesta; Piano Concerto No. 3

Vincent D'Indy. He composes music of strength and open spaces, of powerful forces of nature.

> Symphony on a French Mountain Air; Istar

Sergei Rachmaninoff. This music describes conflict and emergence from depression and sorrow; synthesis of joy and suffering; ultra-Russian essence of melancholy and profound feelings ("We are happy when we are sad"). There is some strong spiritual power and many beautiful melodies.

> The four piano concertos; the three symphonies

Franz von Suppé. This is drama and uplift of the emotions, with very strong energies to dispel moodiness and blocks in the temperament.

> Poet and Peasant; Light Calvary; Boccaccio Overtures

Hector Berlioz. The keynote here is very strongly dramatic and intense, powerful music.

> Te Deum; Requiem; Fantastic Symphony, Harold in Italy; Damnation of Faust; Infancy of Christ; La Marseillaise

Manuel DeFalla. He composes in strong, Spanish melodies and rhythms that often disperse negativity and blockage in the mental-emotional areas.

>Ritual Dance of Fire, The Three-Cornered Hat;
>La Vida Breve; Nights in the Gardens of Spain;
>El Amor Brujo

Jean Sibelius. This is music of the nature devas; strong, removed, at times a-human, but at its best very beautiful, alluring, epic and inspiring. Note the storm feeling in Karelia Overture or the roaring forests of Symphonies No. 1 and 4. Much of Sibelius's music was inspired by ancient Finnish mythology, especially the national epic, *Kalevala.*

>Finlandia; the seven symphonies, Violin Con-
>certo, Swan of Tuonela; En Saga; Oceansides,
>Tapiola; Tempest; The Bard; Karelia

Alexander Glazunov. He composes sparkling nature music (The Seasons) and lyrical yet powerful Russian melodies (Stepan Razin; the symphonies).

EARTH COMPOSERS

This music is less explosive, often calming and con-genial. (Scriabin is an exception.)

Jules Massenet. He composed with deep feeling and emo-tion, rising into strong devotion and spiritual contacts which are often evocations of beautiful landscapes.

>Meditation - Thais; Manon; Alsatian Scenes;
>The Juggler of Notre Dame; Sleep of the Blessed
>Virgin

Arthur Sullivan. Here is music of drama and deep feelings, and of worship. His orchestrations have flare, clarity and strength.

>Te Deum, Irish Symphony; miscellaneous over-
>tures; Gilbert and Sullivan operas

Alexander Scriabin. This is music that is at once strange, other-worldly and hauntingly beautiful in a way that is not human. Cyril Scott in his illuminating work *Music: Its Secret Influence Through the Ages* says that Scriabin's works are often "Deva-music. . .filled with ecstasy and . . . an intense loveliness, but not an earthly loveliness; his music reaches an unutterable grandeur . . . incomparable with anything we have seen or experienced on earth. It is grandeur of mighty Beings, flashing forth Their unimaginable colors and filling the vast expanses with Their song." Nevertheless, though beautiful, this music has not proved uplifting or therapeutic, in my experience.

> Poem of Ecstasy; Divine Poem; Poem of Fire;
> Piano Concerto; piano sonatas

Edward MacDowell. This American composer brings us music of nature that is at once American and also in the nineteenth century European tradition; dramatic music, often with colorful themes.

> The two piano concertos; Celtic Sonata; Indian
> Suite; Woodland Sketches

AIR COMPOSERS

This music is often changeable, bringing frequent shifts in tempo, mood and atmosphere.

Richard Strauss. Strauss' music is moving, but not nearly as deeply and profoundly spiritual as is the best of Wagner's music. It contains strong emotional currents, not always wholesome to the sensitive temperament (example: "Till Eulenspiegel"). Some of his music is very uplifting (Alpine Symphony) and even spiritual, such as *Death and Transfiguration.*

Charles Ives. This music can be discordant but also very beautiful in its more serene moments.

> Symphonies No. 2, 3, 4; The Pond; The
> Celestial Country

Leo Delibes. This is airy, dance-like music, very melodic, that breaks up emotional and mental congestion, while also enlivening the body with its energies.

> Coppélia; Sylvia; Lakmé

Gustav Holst. His music combines melody and warmth with strangeness.

> The Planets; Hymn of Jesus; St. Paul's Suite;
> Festival Te Deum

WATER COMPOSERS

This music often appeals strongly to the emotions and the heart.

Ottorino Respighi. This is a composer of strong melodic and dramatic works, which fill the listener with a many-colored shower of tonal richness. I find Respighi's music enlivening, inspiring and enriching.

> Ancient Dances and Airs; Boticellian Triptych;
> The Birds; The Pines of Rome; The Fountains of
> Rome; The Festivals of Rome; Church Windows

Maurice Ravel. This music often resolves the beautiful and the ugly in watery nature, more than in humanity. Sharp rhythms and pinpointed structure bring a combination of force and feelings, sharp wit and mystery.

> Daphnis and Chloe; piano concertos; Rapsodie
> Espagnole; Pavane for a Dead Princess; In-
> troduction and Allegro; Ship and Ocean

I feel Ravel's "Bolero" is a very harmful piece of music, which should be avoided. The particular rhythms and discord, repeated as they are so often throughout the piece, have the effect on some people of depleting energies and can be very scattering and stressful.

Georges Bizet. This is music of refinement and clear, beautiful melody that is usually therapeutic and vitalizing.

> Symphony in C; Children's Games; Roma;

Patrie Overture; L'Arlesienne Suites; Carmen;
Te Deum

Heitor Villa-Lobos. Here is a very exotic, at times profound music that is reminiscent of the deep South
American forests and jungles. Villa-Lobos's music is alive,
free, at times totally undisciplined, yet at its best colorful
and appealing.

Origin of the Amazon River; Bachianas
Brasileiras 1 through 9; Choros; Forest of the
Amazon; Harp Concerto; Guitar Concerto

Nikolai Rimsky-Korsakov. Listen to the colorful, beautiful
Russian melodies, clothed in exotic instrumental tones—a
sparkling music which often uplifts.

Symphonies No. 1, 2; Scheherazade; Golden
Cockerel; Invisible City of Kitezh; Dubinushka,
Christmas Eve; Russian Easter Overture.

*The real musical genius writes for no other pur-
pose but to express his own Soul, and in so doing, finds life's greatest satisfaction and joy.*
                                        Delius

10

The Deeper Mysteries of Music

In the spheres a wonderful harmony of sound is being produced eternally, and from that Source have all things been created.

Florence Crane

To some it is evident that every sound gives forth a color equivalent. Likewise, the vibratory movements of musical notes and phrases combine to express meaningful patterns or shapings, called *archetypes*, which reside in a super-physical field of thought and feeling. Both the colors and forms of music can be observed clairvoyantly. In addition, some persons "feel" the colors of musical works, and scientific advances have expanded to give us new directions toward demonstrating the colors of music. The Russian composer Alexander Scriabin envisioned a time when a cosmic color organ would reveal simultaneously the colors and formations of every piece of music as it was being played.

The study of the relationship of color animation and sound is called *synesthesia* by some researchers, though the term implies relationships among other senses. I am sure this science will be developed further in our lifetimes. Both Leopold Stokowski, the famed maestro of symphony orchestras, and Walt Disney were interested in the combination of color and sound, and together they produced the great movie classic *Fantasia*, which is an animated union of color, music and movement, a dramatic representation of the energies released through sound and vibration.

Since I as yet do not "see" music colors and forms clairvoyantly, but only feel them, I am very much indebted to the Reverend Flower A. Newhouse, spiritual teacher and Christian mystic, who has shared her valuable insights with me and has described her clairvoyant perception of the colors and musical forms of selections that I have found to be therapeutic for many listeners. I am grateful for the observations shared by another clairvoyant teacher, Geoffrey Hodson in his book *Music Forms:*

> Each note, when sounded or sung, produces...a typical form in superphysical matter. These forms are colored by the way the sound is produced, and the size of the form is decided by the length of time in which a note is sounded or sung...The composer originates and establishes the form, partly by the play of his consciousness during composition and partly by his own performance of the piece.

Music never stands still. Each note and phrase plays its part in building a continuously shifting array of shapes, colors and consistencies which the total piece is vibrating into the listener and his atmosphere. A clairvoyant can describe only the most outstanding color highlights and patterns a musical work is building as it is being played. The composer—by his own thought forms and consciousness during the creation of a piece of music—and the performers who interpret the music together bring through the essence and harmonies of the music originally "heard." Likewise, a sensitive artist or listener, by moving inside the music he is experiencing, can contact mystically the mind and "atmosphere" of the composer. In this way we can understand what Leonard Bernstein meant, during his performance of a Mahler symphony, when he said, "But I AM Gustav Mahler."

The more reverently and expectantly you can experience a piece of music, the more its mysterious beauty and hidden essences will open to you, revealing far greater depth and power.

I want to share with you a list of some musical selections, as viewed clairvoyantly by F. A. Newhouse, for their colors and patterns of form. Consider these descriptions with open mind and heart, allowing the music—hereafter—to bathe you and fill you with its own distinctive color potencies and archetypal patterns.

Beethoven - Fifth Symphony: Here is royal purple, interwoven with saffron—his music comes forth like great waves that envelop an audience.

Elgar - Pomp and Circumstance March, No. 1: The highlight is flame and yellow hues; these colors for a time circulate like waves that fold into one another. Then, in the center of these waving colors appears an archetype somewhat resembling a beacon or torch. Gradually, this figure begins to unfurl what looks like a large white streaming flag. From this flag emanate other white flags, unfurling notes on either side of the central figure. This music is an ordination piece from the angelic kingdom, according to Rev. Newhouse.

Tchaikovsky - Andante (from Swan Lake, Act 2, Dance of the Swans): There are beams of golden light; harp tones create bursts of light whose colors are outside our spectrum.

J. S. Bach - A Mighty Fortress: There are yellow waves of power moving out into the atmosphere, forming an anvil-like figure.

Liszt - Liebestraum: This music looks like smoke waves—a feminine figure moves in white at the center; there are purple and some rose, with aqua during the dance-like tunes.

Schubert - Ave Maria: Another clairvoyant-teacher, Corrine Heline, in her book *The Cosmic Harp*, describes the color of this music as primarily "rose-lavender—the synthesis of love and sorrow."

Debussy - Clair de lune: There are saffron and pink, with a fountain-like figure spraying power; also, a pan-pipe giving forth opalescent bubbles.

Herbert - Ah, Sweet Mystery of Life: A chalice in gold is emanating golden beams; hands held upwards, move toward the chalice—rose streams flow.

Gounod - Sanctus (from Saint Cecilia Mass): Rev. Newhouse feels that Gounod may be from the Deva line. This piece sends forth rose tones which blend into pink; other colors are orchid and white.

Goin' Home (Negro spiritual): There is an orange hill, with a male figure climbing; also, apricot hues.

Silent Night: This creates pink shades, like camellias; some petals are deep rose, others are more pink.

Sibelius - Finlandia: Here is a Deva strain, blessing the earth with spiritual incitements. The music brings in mystic streams of orchid and white, rinsing through the earth and continuously emitting bright green beams. (No wonder that this stirring piece awoke the Finns to patriotic resistance against Russian invasion!)

O Holy Night: This is an Archangel call; the crystal light of the higher world is mingling with green coming from the earth.

Mine Eyes Have Seen the Glory: The colors are green and white like plumes of fiery power; heavenly choirs are descending to bless. The plumes change into an archetype of the American flag. According to Rev. Newhouse, this piece is the Planetary Logos' baptism of the earth.

Grieg - Nocturne (from Lyric Suite): There are silver, shimmering sea green waves of power; an angel of the night blesses nature's many forms of life.

Piano Concerto (2nd movement): There are waves of blue, splashed with a rose color that contains some burgundy tints; large thought forms appear like great cornucopias, with flowing, seed-like shapes of shining, varied colors.

I Love Thee (song): Here are thought forms of hearts and praying hands, against a rose background; bursts of golden flashing colors.

Rachmaninoff - Piano Concerto No. 2 (Finale): The triumphal theme reveals earthians moving up upon a varicolored mountain toward resplendent light.

Chopin - Nocturne, Op. 9, No. 2: Special notes create a turning bell-like music form of peach, that spins around in unison with the music; latter part has blue mist veiling bright forms which dance through veils into openness and continue to rotate all about the atmosphere.

Deep River (Negro spiritual): Deep blue currents move through the atmosphere horizontally; midway through the piece appears a gold-domed city, shining above the azure waves (the city represents one view of Paradise, on the inner planes).

Malotte - The Lord's Prayer: Blue tones; slowly an archetype of a white altar takes form; leaning against the altar are two large, praying hands; at the end of the piece only the praying hands remain—all blue and orchid have disappeared.

Humperdinck - Children's Prayer (from Hansel and Gretel): Great reservoirs of light, one giving rise to another in fountain-like bursts of creation; at last, one glorious stream of light emerges from the base of the fountain and lifts the prayers originating in men up to God. The towering column of light keeps ascending, and as it does, the base of the fountain rises and widens, becoming more luminous and expansive.

Franck - Panis Angelicus: This is a blue piece; blue waves, with a lily-like archetype are facing downard in the beginning, fluidic, then later they turn upward. Three-quarters of the way through the piece, bell-shaped tones appear. Blue tones resolve, like sunset and light blue.

Insights into the colors and forms of great music help me to feel more deeply the great beauty of shapes and colors that inspired music delivers powerfully into our atmosphere. I look forward to the day in the future when more persons will be able to "see" into great music and in this way will be able to share its healing energies with others. I am grateful to Reverend Newhouse for sharing her visions.

11

cMusic for The Future

> *In the education of the future, music for every person will be deemed as necessary as the reading and writing at present, for it will be clearly seen that it is a most powerful means for bringing life, health and strength.*
>
> Prentice Mulford, *Thought Forces*

Originally, music was the testimony of the human soul. It was an integral part of the life of the community. Laws of harmony were followed, and only music, not "noise," was allowed into a society. As each person added his stone to the building of the great cathedral, so everyone's "tone" contributed to the evolving melody of man's world. But with the rise of individualism, many egos went their own ways, living for themselves alone, thus producing chaos in the world. Now, in the final years of the twentieth century, we move toward synthesis. Just to survive, man, woman and child must help each other. We must come together more constructively and lovingly, and great music can help us to move in this direction.

Today we are realizing once again the potential power of beautiful music to integrate the personality and temperament, to awaken us to the soul, and to link us to supernal forces of Light that surround us. It is becoming increasingly clear again that great music inspires us, relieves our tensions and strengthens our lives. To be fed by beautiful music is a necessity.

The finest music is transforming; it unlocks creativity. Once, while teaching a class in creative writing, I played a piece of music and witnessed a man suddenly shout for joy because a certain musical phrase helped to "bring through" the ending to a short story which he had tried to finish for seven years. I recall a woman artist who painted great angels moving in Light as she listened to the full-volume chorus from Haydn's *Creation*. And I recall, gratefully, the inspiring workshop of Alignment Through Music, led by Director Kay Ortmans at Well-Springs (in Ben Lomond, California) in which the therapeutic energies of music were combined with movement, drawing with pastels, and massage.

Great music is also exciting: it heightens feelings, enhances life's scenes and deepens relationships. It is thrilling to notice how many movie makers are now turning more to the great classics for inspiration for their scenes and soundtracks. Here are some examples:

> Somewhere in Time - Rachmaninoff
> Fantasia - J. S. Bach; Dukas; Ponchielli;
>   Beethoven; Schubert; Mussorgsky; Tchaikovsky
> Song of Norway - Grieg
> 2001, Space Odyssey - Johann Strauss; Ligeti;
>   Richard Strauss
> Clockwork Orange - Beethoven; Mahler
> Turning Point - Tchaikovsky; Wieniawski;
>   Prokofiev
> Death in Venice - Mahler
> Elvira Madigan - Mozart
> Interlude - Albinoni
> Kramer Vs. Kramer - Purcell; Vivaldi
> A Little Romance - Vivaldi
> Requiem for a Heavyweight (T.V. production) -
>   Sibelius

Apocalypse Now - Wagner
Excalibur - Wagner; Orff
Four Seasons - Vivaldi
Elephant Man - Barber
Barry Lyndon - Handel
So Fine - Wagner and Verdi
All the Marbles - Leoncavallo

We also notice several contemporary composers who are producing some of their finest creations for film soundtracks. Among my favorites are Lee Holdridge (*Other Side of the Mountain*, Part 2, *Forever Young, Forever Free, Jonathan Livingston Seagull, Jesus and Lazarus*); Maurice Jarre (*Ryan's Daughter, Shogun, Doctor Zhivago*); Georges Delerue (*Promise at Dawn, King of Hearts, A Little Romance*); John Barry (*Somewhere in Time, Born Free, The Dove*); and Bernard Herrmann. The soundtracks for the movies just mentioned contain many beautiful melodies and emanate healing energies. My own personal favorite remains *Sound of Music* by Rodgers and Hammerstein.

Today, we are just waking up to the incredible potency of great music and what it can mean to our lives. The possibilities of music as a healing force are enormous. I believe that in the coming years, great music sensitively and perceptively used will prove to be a major catalyst to better health and well-being—in homes, at places of work, in hospitals, schools, stores, shopping malls, penal institutions, for mothers' birthing, language study, and in the creative arts.

In these final decades of the twentieth century, we are beginning to rediscover how powerfully the currents of beautiful music can enter our bones and consciousness. Like a "healing salve," inspired melodies and sound vibrations can unlock cramps and blockage in our physical, emotional and mental layers. Even beyond these areas, great music stirs tingles in our souls, causing us to open our hearts to life's larger, eternal horizons.

I believe that eventually great music will be more widely accepted as the greatest art form, for it truly contains unlimited powers of transformation for each person. Music is always moving and becoming, and it carries us beyond our boundaries. It is the healing lubricant for Good which brings us into closer union with our work, our friendships, and our Creator. The finest music opens our hearts and minds, wielding a magnetism capable of joining together groups and masses of humanity. True music inspires persons to live more unselfishly, in greater kindness to each other and in fuller service to God and his Creation.

I Am Music

I am Music, most ancient of the arts. I am more than ancient; I am eternal. Even before life began upon this earth, I was here—in the winds and the waves. When the first trees and flowers and grasses appeared, I was among them. And when Man came, I at once became the most delicate, most subtle and most powerful medium for the expression of Man's emotions.

When men were little better than beasts, I influenced them for their good. In all ages I have inspired men with hope, kindled their love, given a voice to their joys, cheered them on to valorous deeds, and soothed them in times of despair. I have played a great part in the drama of life, whose end and purpose is the complete perfection of Man's nature. Through my influence, human nature has been uplifted, sweetened and refined. With the aid of men, I have become a Fine Art. I have a myriad of voices and instruments. I am in the hearts of all men and on their tongues, in all lands among all peoples; the ignorant and unlettered know me, not less than the rich and the learned. For I speak to all men, in a language that all understand. Even the deaf hear me, if they but listen to the voices of their own souls. I am the food of love. I have taught men gentleness and peace: and I have led them onward to heroic deeds. I comfort the lonely, and I harmonize the discord of crowds. I am a necessary luxury to all men. I am MUSIC.

Anonymous

ᴄᴀppendix ᴄA
Music for Stress Reduction, Relaxation and Focus

New Age Selections

Patrick Ball - Celtic Harp; From a Distant Time; Secret Isles

Kim Robertson - Moonrise; Water Spirit; Wind Shadows I, II; Celtic Christmas

Stevan Pasero - Winter Heartsongs for Guitar; Nutcracker Suite (Guitar)

Bruce Becvar - Take It to Heart

Alex Jones - Kali's Dream; Pranava

Mike Rowland - The Fairy Ring; Solace; Silver Wings

Max Highstein - The Healer's Touch

Patrick DiVietri - Partita Teresiana; Invocation

William Aura - Lovely Day

Tom Barabas - Magic in December; You're the End of the Rainbow

Evenson - High Joy; Peaceful Pond; Whistling Woodhearts; Tropic of Paradise

Jim Chappell - Dusk

Spencer Brewer - Emerald

Liz Storey - Solid Colors

Carolyn Margrete - Emerald Season

Aoliah - Majesty

Daniel Kobialka - Path of Joy; Sunspace; Journeys in Time; Goin' Home

Classical Selections and Miscellaneous

Dvorak - Silent Woods; Cello Concerto

Vaughan-Williams - Lark Ascending

Beethoven - Symphony No. 6

J. S. Bach - Jesu, Joy of Man's Desiring; Sheep May Safely Graze

Handel - Largo (From Xerxes); Water Music

Mozart - Flute and Piano Concertos

Pachelbel - Canon in D

Vivaldi - The Four Seasons; Miscellaneous Concertos

Corelli - Concerti Grossi

Grieg - Holberg Suite; "Morning" (from Peer Gynt)

Mendelssohn - Song without Words

Rodrigo - Aranjuez Concerto

cAppendix B

The following lists of musical selection describe further the suggestions contained in the book's individual chapters. I have enlarged the total number, and with each piece I have attempted to include the artists/conductors and labels of the renditions I have found most helpful.

1. Chiefly Classical Masterpieces

Addinsell - Warsaw Concerto (Adni, Alwyn—Angel SZ-37757)
Stirring piece; romantic; inspired by the tragedies and losses of war; good for emotional release.

Albéniz, Isaac - Suite Española (Fruhbeck de Burgos—London 6581)
Pictorial music of Spain; lovely melodies; awakens feelings and imagination.

Anderson, Leroy - Sleigh Ride; Bugler's Holiday; Typewriter; Syncopated Clock (Fennell—Mercury 75013)
Activates body, emotions and mind; clear rhythms and melodies.

Bacarisse - Concerto for Guitar & Orchestra (Yepes, Alonso—DGG-2530326)
Slow middle movement ideal for contemplation and meditation.

Bach, Johann Sebastian - Toccata and Fugue in D (Stokowski—Seraphim S-60235; London 21096)
A cosmic experience; great expanse; powerful and majestic; good for cleansing and lifting spirits.

_____. Brandenburg Concertos (Casals—Columbia M2S-731)
Extremely exhilarating; delightful colors and tones; moves the listener to deeper levels of focus, clarity and universal life flow.

_____. Come Sweet Death (Stokowski—Seraphim
S-60235; Fox, organ—Westminster Gold-WGS-8145)

Caressing, embracing and beautiful, this music of understanding and
unconditional love is extremely therapeutic; aids relaxation and meditation.

_____. Violin Concertos (Szeryng, Marriner—Philips
9500226)

Good for mental focus and poise.

_____. Two Concertos for Two Pianos (R. & G.
Casadesus, Kuentz—Odyssey 32160382)

Music of warmth and dignity; inspirational and centering.

_____. Jesu, Joy of Man's Desiring (Flagstad, vocal—Lon-
don OS-25141; Marriner—Angel S-37443)

Music of spiritual devotion; opens heart center and awakens aspiration.

_____. A Bach Program (Stokowski—RCA AGL1-3656;
Ormandy—Columbia MS-7405, choral)

Marvelous samplers of Bach's music that awaken a variety of emotions
and inner responses; this is music of universal joy and compassion,
opening the listener to God's grandeur.

_____. Goldberg Variations, Harpsichord
(Landowska—RCA VIC-1650)

Elegant and refreshing.

Bantock, Sir Granville - Hebridean Symphony (Heald,
Smith—Gough and Davy GD2002; available through International Records, Box 1140, Goleta, CA 93116)

Prompts creativity and emotional response; lovely melodies and
varieties in mood.

Barber, Samuel - Adagio for Strings (Munch—RCA
AGL1-3790; I Musici—Philips Festivo 6570181)

Restful and meditative, feeling oriented; rises to crescendo and calms to
silence.

_____. Second Essay for Orchestra; Scene from Shelley
(Golschmann—Vanguard 2083)

Dramatic music, excellent for creative arts and pictorial / visualization
work; also useful for emotional release and catharsis.

Beethoven - Symphony No. 5 (Furtwangler—Heliodor
HS25078; Kleiber—DGG 2530516)

In places deeply stirring and in others reflective; awakens courage to
overcome.

_____. Symphony No. 6, Pastorale (Reiner—RCA
LSC-2614; Furtwangler—EMI label; Klemperer—Angel
S-35711)

First two movements especially good for emotional cleansing and upliftment; joyful; storm movement, followed by "Hymn of Thanksgiving,"
also quite rewarding.

_____. Symphony No. 9, Choral (Furtwangler—Seraphim
2B-6068; Reiner—RCA LSC-3316

Music that paints the creation out of the void and culminates in the
magnificent "Hymn to Brotherhood", inspires universal love and
understanding among nations; third movement meditative and serene.

_____. Piano Concerto No. 5, Emperor (Novaes,
Perlea—Vox 511930; Katchen, Gamba—London
STS-15210)

Inspires courage and joy; energizing and uplifting piece; middle movement is serene and angelic.

_____. Violin Concerto (Francescatti, Walter—Odyssey
Y-30042; Mutter, Karajan—DGG 2531250)

Another therapeutic piece; soulful melodies strong in energy.

_____. Choral Fantasy for Piano and Chorus and
Orchestra (Katchen, Gamba—London STS-15211)

Stirring and empowering; finale expresses joy and high velocity.

_____. String Quartet, Opus 131 (Bernstein—DGG
2531-077)

Exalted; orchestral harmonies majestic and centering; good for reflection.

Berlioz - Harold in Italy (Suk, Fischer-Dieskau—
Quintessence 7103)

Music of wide emotional range; at times peaceful and melodic, but with
manic moments romantic in melodic content.

_____. Symphonie fantastique (Freccia—Quintessence
7057; Martinon—Angel S-37138)

Pictorial music; describes inner workings of man in love and his ecstasy
and agony for his beloved; third movement, "Scenes in the Country,"
especially lovely.

_____. Te Deum (Davis—Philips 839790); Requiem
(Simoneau, Munch—RCA VICS-6043)

Powerful, sacred choral music containing many emotional
extremes.

Bizet - Symphony in C (Martinon—DGG 2535238;
Beecham—Seraphim S-60192)

Elegant and rhythmically enlivening; good for both energizing and reverie.

_____. Carmen, Selections (Beecham—Seraphim S-60134);
L'Arlesienne Suite (Markevitch—Philips Festivo 6570107)

Enlivening and uplifting with strong rhythms in places.

Bloch - Schelomo (Piatigorsky, Munch—RCA
AGL1-4086)

Brooding, emotional piece; in sections prophetic and powerful; good for reflection and feeling response.

_____. Baal Shem; Abodah, God's Worship (Mordkovitch,
Gerhardt—RCA RL-25370)

Reflective, devotional music.

_____. Sacred Service (Bernstein—Columbia MS-6221)

Joyous and mighty.

Boccherini - Guitar Quintets (P. Romero, Marriner—Philips 9500985; 9500789; 9500621)

Beautiful, pleasant melodies; good for centering; awaken joyfulness.

Bois-Vallée - Adagio Religioso (Bonneau—Philips
6511-001)

Devotional, quiet and reassuring.

Borodin - Symphony No. 2 (Svetlanov—Quintessence
7165)

Singularly Russian, exploring feelings of power, mystery, movement and triumph.

_____. Nocturne for String Orchestra
(Stokowski—Seraphim S-60278)

Peaceful, good for relieving stress; engenders calmness.

Brahms - Symphony No. 1 (Furtwangler—DGG
2530-744; Walter—Odyssey Y-30311; Païta—Lodia
LOD-779)

Solid and earthy, yet tender and warm; final movement moves toward climax, crescendo and release; good for emotional/mental cleansing.

_____. Symphony No. 2 (Monteux—Philips Festivo
6570108; Furtwangler—Unicorn or EMI import)

Brahms' nature symphony; at times very dramatic.

_____. Piano Concerto No. 1 (Fleisher, Szell—Odyssey
Y-31273; Gilels, Jochum—DGG 2530258)

Extremely stirring music; finale especially conducive to emotional clearance and uplift.

_____. Piano Concerto No. 2 (Richter, Maazel—Angel RL-32041; Fleisher, Szell—Odyssey Y-32222)

One of the greatest piano concertos ever composed; at times deeply reflective while at others eruptive and volcanic; quiet third movement especially for devotion.

_____. Lullaby (Robles, harp—Argo ZK61)

Especially warm piece of music; simple and healing.

Britten - Four Sea Interludes, from Peter Grimes (Giulini—Angel S-36215)

Tone pictures of the sea; in some places stirring, in others pensive and brooding; activates both physical and emotional natures.

Bruch - Violin Concerto; Scottish Fantasy (Perlman, Lopez-Cobos—Angel S-37210; Chung, Kempe—London 6795)

Melodic and inspiring, emotionally uplifting.

_____. Concerto for Two Pianos and Orchestra (Berkofsky and Twining, Dorati—Angel S-36997)

Expansive to the feelings; gorgeous melodies.

Bruckner - Symphony No. 3 (Szell—Columbia MS-6897)

Inbreakings of light.

_____. Symphony No. 4, Romantic (Jochum—DGG 2535111; Barenboim—DGG 2530336); Symphony No. 8 (Van Beinum—Epic SC-6011; Bohm—DGG 2709068); Symphony No. 9 (Giulini—Angel S-37287)

Music of devotion and expansive consciousness; the 8th Symphony is linked to the Archangel Michael and describes the conquest of evil by forces of Light.

Butterworth - A Shropshire Lad; The Banks of Green Willow; Two English Idylls (Marriner—Argo ZRG-860)

Atmospheric music that paints pastoral scenes; mostly quieting to the emotions.

Byrd - Mass in Four Parts; Mass in Five Parts (Preston—Argo ZRG-858)

Celestial, devotional music; brings feelings of great majesty and connects listener with upward spiral of life.

Canning - Fantasy on a Hymn of Justin Morgan (Stokowski—Everest SDBR-3070)

Peaceful; inspiring American flavor.

Canteloube - Songs of the Auvergne (De Los Angeles,
Jacquillat—Angel S-36897; 36898)
A wide range of music including lively songs, love songs of mellow
flavor, and pastoral scenes of French countryside; energizing; awakens
feelings.

Carlstedt, Jan - Symphony of Brotherhood
(Westerberg—EMI 055-34424)
Composed in memory of Martin Luther King, Jr.; at times very serious
and elegiac; contains a nobility and dignity.

Celibidache - Pocket Garden (Intercord 160.832)
Good for fantasy and creativity.

Castelnuovo-Tedesco - Guitar Concerto in D (Williams,
Ormandy—Columbia MS-6834)
Strong Spanish flavor; highly melodic and rhythmically pleasing;
energizing.

Catalani - Loreley: Dance of the Water Nymphs
(Toscanini—RCA VIC-1263)
Marvelously pictorial and scintillating; evokes imagination and move-
ment.

Chabrier - Orchestral Works: España, Festival Polonaise,
etc. (Froment—Turnabout 34671)
Light music that airs out the system; good for light moments; parts are
energizing.

Chaminade, Cecile - Concertino for Flute and Orchestra
(Galway, Dutoit—RCA ARL1-3777)
Pleasing music for flute; emotionally stimulating.

Charpentier, Marc-Antoine - Midnight Mass
(Willcocks—Angel S-36528)
Reverent and inspiring.

Chausson - Symphony in B-flat; Festival Evening
(Plasson—Seraphim S-60310)
Dramatic and reflective; may lift one out of melancholy.

Chavez - Sinfonia India (Bernstein—Columbia MS-6514)
Exotic, stimulating, celebrational.

Chopin - Andante Spianato and Grande Polonaise
(Brendel—Vanguard C-10058; Zimerman, Giulini—DGG
2531126)
Spiritually elevating; brings about deep feeling and aspiration.

_____. Piano Concerto No. 1 (Simon, Beissel—Vox
SVBX-5126)

Positive energy flow with profoundly meditative slow movement; elevates mood.

_____. Waltzes (Lipatti—Odyssey Y-32160058;
Simon—Turnabout 34580)
Provide wonderful release for energy; activate physical body and emotional nature.

Clementi - Sonatas for Piano (Horowitz—RCA
ARM1-3689)
Good for mental focus and stability; enlivening and centering; build sense of order.

Cooke, Arnold - Concerto for Clarinet and String
Orchestra (King, Melsted—Hyperion A66031)
Some lovely pastoral flavors here; mellowness allows for centering and good feeling.

Copland - Appalachian Spring (Copland—RCA
LSC-2401); Billy the Kid (Johanos—Turnabout 34169);
Old American Songs (Warfield, Copland—Columbia
MS-6497); Lincoln Portrait, Sandburg
(Kostelanetz—Columbia CSP-91A02007); Quiet City
(Copland—Columbia MS-7375)
Uniquely American music; many beautiful melodies; dramatic, reflective and devotional times as well; energy raisers; also good for imagination and for building feeling of well-being.

Corelli - Concerti grossi (I Musici—Philips Festivo
6770023)
Stabilizing music with lovely melodies and pleasing flavor; for mental poise and order.

Debussy - Engulfed Cathedral (Stokowski—London
21006)
Arousing deep memories of another age, perhaps the lost continent of Atlantis; music that pulls the listener in; stimulates creative imagination.

_____. Clair de lune (Ormandy—Columbia MS-6883)
Nostalgic, calls up feelings of reverie.

_____. The Sea, La Mer (Munch—RCA VICS-1041;
Boulez—Columbia MS-7361; Bernstein—Columbia
MS-6754)
Marvelously pictorial, suggestive scenes; right for emotional release; brings power and mystery.

_____. Nocturnes (Boulez—Columbia M-30483;
Abbado—DGG 2530038)

Mysterious and evocative pieces; "Festivals" is a particularly energetic piece that activates the body and feelings.

_____. Prelude to the Afternoon of a Faun
(Monteux—London STS-15356; Thomas—DGG 2530145)
Expansive and reflective, at times rising to heights of reverie and winsomeness; for relieving heaviness and lethargy.

_____. Sacred and Profane Dances for Harp and
Orchestra (Cotelle, Markevitch—DGG 2535325)
Again, the sounds of another world, mysterious and alluring; the harp penetrates with its exotic melodies.

Delalande - Symphonies for the King's Suppers (DGG
ARC-198333)
Stimulating and festive; music for brass and orchestra.

Delibes - Coppelia (Mari—Angel S-3843); Sylvia
(Mari—Angel S-3860)
Beautifully melodic, enlivening music; good for movement and energy.

Delius - On Hearing the First Cuckoo in Spring
(Beecham—Seraphim S-60185)
Very calming and centering nature music.

_____. Florida Suite (Beecham—Seraphim S-60212)
Musical picture of the beauty of 19th century Florida coast, depicting night on the river and the echoes of Negro songs mixing with the fragrance of orange groves; wonderful for reverie and reflection.

_____. Summer Night on the River; Song Before Sunrise;
La Calinda; In a Summer Garden (Barbirolli—Angel
S-36588)
More beautiful, atmospheric music; good for creative imagination.

Dello Joio - Triumph of Saint Joan Symphony (Columbia
CSP AML-4615)
Dramatic and containing powerful energies of overcoming.

Dinicu, Heifetz - Hora Staccato (Gamley—Quintessence
PMC-7069)
Exhilarating and vibrant piece.

Dvořák - Amid Nature; Carnival (Kertesz—Vox
SVBX-5138); Czech Suite (Mackerras—Philips 6500203)
Slavic delights, depicting festive flavors and a strong feeling for nature; good energy raisers.

_____. Cello Concerto (Fournier, Szell—DGG 2535106;
Rostropovich, Karajan—DGG 139044)
Melodious, noble and inspiring; help for the feelings.

____. Symphony No. 8 (Walter—Odyssey Y-33231;
Marriner—Philips 6514050)
A nature painting in melody; uplifts the spirits; energizing and lyrical.

____. Symphony No. 9, From the New World
(Walter—Odyssey Y-30045; Kertesz—London STS-15101)
A description of the magic and beautiful sights of a new world; combines American Indian-like tunes with Slavonic flavors and stirring melodies; uplifts.

____. Slavonic Dances (Szell—Odyssey Y2-33524)
Moving rhythms and lovely colors enliven the listener.

Elgar - Enigma Variations (Monteux—London STS-15188;
Boult—Angel S-36799)
Varied musical portraits of the composer's friends; some of the music bubbles and is powerful; other sections are more pensive and quiet, such as "Nimrod," ninth variation.

____. Sea Pictures (Baker, Barbirolli—Angel S-36796)
Songs of power and devotion with sea (orchestra) accompanying; nostalgic in places and inspiring.

____. Starlight Express (Handley—EMI TC2-ESDW 711)
Music of variety; some sections energetic and songful, others more quiet; good for creative imagination.

Enesco - Roumanian Rhapsodies (Dorati—Mercury
75018)
Stirring music, sparkling in melody and rhythmic vitality; good for movement and physical stimulation.

van Eyck - Der Fluyten Lust-Hof (Kosofsky—Titanic 1)
Transparent music for solo recorder; excellent for clearance and relief of stress; also to be played while eating.

Falla - Nights in the Gardens of Spain (Rubinstein,
Jorda—RCA LSC-2430; Haskil, Markevitch—Philips
Festivo SFM-23025)
Scenes of mystery and nocturnal, haunting melodies; marvelous for painting and imagination.

Fanshawe, David - African Sanctus (Philips 6558001)
Unique piece of music, brings in great energy and exotic, spontaneous singing in praise; also filled with nature sounds; stimulates the system; good for body movement, dance and singing.

Fauré - Requiem (Willcocks—Seraphim S-60096)
Reverent; excellent for deepening devotion.

Finzi, Gerald - Intimations of Immortality
(Handley—Lyrita SRCS-75)
Poetic musical journey; deepens aspiration. (See Wordsworth's poem by the same title.)

____. Cello Concerto (Ma, Handley—Lyrita SRCS-112)
Lyrical and moving.

Foster - Songs (Smith, Gregg Singers—Turnabout 34609)
Arousing friendliness and warmth; good for awakening feelings.

Franck, César - The Beatitudes (Schwann AMS-4504-5)
Music of praise, love, and devotion.

____. Symphony in D-minor (Monteux—RCA
ATL1-4156; Hampton, solo organ—Musical Heritage
MHS-3570)
Music of deep aspiration and spiritual beauty; good for solitary listening experience.

____. Panis angelicus (Pavarotti—London OS5-26473)
Angelic, exquisitely devotional; uplifting.

____. Psyche (Strauss—Connoisseur Society C-4009)
Music of mystery and expansive beauty; good for increasing imagination and poetic sensitivity.

Fučik - Marches (Neumann—Quintessence PMC-7038)
Stirring and enlivening; stimulates physical body.

Gabrieli - Music for Brass and Organ (Biggs,
Burgin—Columbia MS-6117)
Stirring and stimulating to body and emotions.

Gershwin - Concerto in F; Rhapsody in Blue
(Previn—Angel S-36810; Entremont, Ormandy—
Columbia MS-7013)
Jazzy and not terribly therapeutic in spots, but in others lovely melodies that inspire the emotions.

Giuliani, Mauro - Concertos for Guitar and Strings
(P. Romero, Marriner—Philips 9500320; 6500918)
Very uplifting, beautiful melodies and harmonious sounds; good for any time.

Gluck - Dance of the Blessed Spirits
(Stokowski—Seraphim S-60278)
Gorgeous and uplifting; music of joy and peace that clears the atmosphere.

Gounod - St. Cecilia Mass, especially Sanctus
(Hartemann—Angel S-36214)
Music of devotional fervor and aspiration; very powerful in sections;
good for release.

_____. Unfold Ye Portals of Creation (Condie,
Ormandy—Columbia MS-6367)
Powerful; good for release and spiritual aspiration.

Grieg - Piano Concerto in A (Lupu, Previn—London
6840; Curzon, Fjeldstad—London STS-15407; Zimerman,
Karajan—DGG 3302043)
Perhaps the greatest piano concerto ever composed in the sense of its
balance and total beauty; powerful outer movements with heavenly
slow movement in the middle; a total experience.

_____. Holberg Suite (Flagello—Peters PCE-035)
Varied moods; mostly lyrical and awakening deep memories.

_____. Peer Gynt (Hollweg, Beecham—Angel RL-32026)
Tonal palette with many colors and melodies recalling Scandinavian
landscape and folksongs; also nature beings.

Griffes - Three Poems of Fiona MacLeod; Golden
Peacock; Pleasure Dome of Kubla Khan (Ozawa—New
World 273)
Impressionistic and poetic pieces; mysterious and exotic.

Grigny - Hymns for Organ, solo (Isoir—Musical Heritage
Society MHS-6079)
Reverent and inspiring in a private way; requires "getting into."

Grofé - Grand Canyon Suite (Cash, Kostelanetz—
Columbia BT-13561; Ormandy—Columbia MS-6003)
Pictorial and evocative music; good for imagination; stimulates physical
body.

Handel - Harp Concerto, Opus 4, No. 6 (Zabaleta,
Kuentz—DGG 139304)
Elegant, centering; nice while eating.

_____. Israel in Egypt (Mackerras—DGG ARC-2708020)
Lovely choral sections that inspire spiritually.

_____. Messiah (Hogwood—Oiseau D189D3;
Sargent—Seraphim S-6056; Davis—Philips Sc71Ax300)
Music of deep adoration and praise to the Christ; Handel believed this
music was "given to him" and he never charged for a single performance; attunes the listener spiritually to the Christ and the angels.

_____. Water Music (Van Beinum—Philips Festivo
6570171; Harnoncourt—Telefunken 6.42497)
Sparkling melodies and rhythms; good for cleansing and artistic creativity.

_____. Let the Bright Seraphim, from Samson (Te
Kanawa, Willcocks—BBC-REP 413)
Joyful song of praise; very energizing.

Haydn, Franz Joseph - Piano Concertos (Alpenheim,
Dorati—Vox SVBX-5136); Trumpet Concerto (Stringer,
Marriner—London STS-15546); The Creation (Mar-
riner—Philips 6769047); the Masses (miscellaneous
labels); Symphonies (Dorati—London)
Music that breathes with sparkle and vitality; excellent "up" music; good also for mental centering and clarity.

Heenan - A Maori Suite (Heenan—Kiwi SLC-72)
Exotic piece arousing love, devotion, action and aspiration.

Herbert, Victor - Ah, Sweet Mystery of Life (Sills,
Kostelanetz—Angel SFO-37160)
"For 'tis love, and love alone, the world is seeking / And 'tis love, and love alone that can repay! / 'Tis the answer, 'tis the end and all of living. / For it is love alone that rules for aye!"

_____. American Fantasia (Kunzel—Turnabout
TV-34714)
Another beautiful, melodic and inspiring piece of Americana.

Hill, Alfred - Symphony, The Joy of Life (Australian
Festival of Music, vol. 1, SFC-80018)
Music that lifts the listener into greater feelings of devotion and power.

Hindemith - Mathis der maler, Symphony
(Steinberg—DGG 2530246)
Awakens reverence and imagination.

Holst - Jupiter, from The Planets (Boult—Angel S-36420)
"Jupiter" is very refreshing; the other movements are varied in mood.

Honegger - Summer Pastorale (Bernstein—Columbia
MS-6659)
A quiet, lyrical piece portraying a time and scene in nature.

Hovhaness, Alan - Mysterious Mountain (Reiner—RCA
AGL1-4215)
A beautiful meditative experience; takes listener into private worlds of melody and tonal landscape; good for deep meditation.

_____. Magnificat (Whitney—Poseidon 1018)
Inspires joy and rapture in the Divine Presence; synthesis of East and West in style and descriptive content.

_____. Talin (Sobol, Flagello—Peters PLE-071)
Piece for clarinet and strings that is introspective in most places; quieting to the emotions.

_____. And God Created Great Whales
(Kostelanetz—Columbia M-30390)
Combines actual whale songs with a shimmering orchestral background; great for imagination.

Hummel - Mandolin Concerto (Hladky—Turnabout TV
340035)
Soothing and good for centering.

D'Indy - Symphony on a French Mountain Air
(Casadesus, Ormandy—Odyssey Y-31274)
Suggestive of Alpine scenes, at times with great power and at others ruminative; inspires creativity and relieves lethargy.

Ireland, John - The Holy Boy (Dilkes—EMI ESD-7101)
Reverent and quieting.

Jánaček - Sinfonietta (Ančerl—Quintessence 7184;
Ozawa—Angel S-36045)
Brassy, celebrational music; activates body and emotions.

_____. Slavonic (or Glagolitic) Mass (Kubelik—DGG
138954)
Music of praise; stirring and majestic; good for releasing anger. The composer's description of it is:

> Always the scent of the woods—that was the
> incense. I felt a cathedral grow out of the
> giant expanse of the woods and the sky
> stretching far into the misty distance.
>
> A flock of white sheep were ringing the bells.
> Now I hear the voice of each archpriest in
> tenor solo, a maiden angel in the soprano
> and in the choir our people.
>
> The tall firs, their tips lit up by
> the stars, are the candles and during
> the ceremony I see the vision of Saint
> Wenceslas, and I hear the language of
> the missionaries, Cyril and Methodius.

Jongen - Symphonie Concertante for Organ and
Orchestra (Fox, Pretre—Angel S-36984)
A real showpiece for drama of organ and orchestra; highly stirring in places, meditative and reflective in others; stimulates whole person; spiritually elevating.

Joplin - Piano Music (Rifkin—Nonesuch 73026)
Moving rhythms; activates body.

Josten - Sacred Concerto I-II (Stokowski—CRI S-200)
Exceptional piece, notable for its colors and exotic rhythms;
intriguing.

Kabalevsky - The Comedians (Kondrashin—RCA
LSC-2398)
Buoyant, energizing and pleasing.

Ketelbey - In a Monastery Garden; Bells Across the
Meadow (Lanchbery—Angel S-37483)
Simple, appealing music with pleasing melodies; awakens nostalgia.

Khachaturian - Sabre Dance, from Gayne
(Khachaturian—Angel S-37411)
Exciting and high voltage, enlivening the physical body; good for fast
movement and dancing.

Kodaly - Hary Janos Suite (Szell—Columbia MS-7408)
Exotic sounds of the cymbalon combine with orchestral colors;
stimulating to imagination.

Korngold - Violanta, Prelude and Carnival
(Horenstein—Quintessence PMC-7047)
Exuberant, enlivening music; strong melodies.

_____. Violin Concerto (Perlman, Previn—Angel
DS-37770)
Highly melodic and romantic; good for feelings.

_____. Garden Scene (Sakonov—London SPC-21089)
Richly warm and melodic serenade of love.

Kreisler - Violin Music (Elman—Vanguard 367;
Perlman—Angel S-37171; 37254; 37630)
Charming melodies exuding a warmth and friendliness; good for in-
timacy and developing friendship.

Krumpholz - Sonata in D for Flute and Harp (Bis-143)
Especially refreshing; beneficial to play for children.

Lalo - Symphonie espagnole (Kyung-Wha Chung,
Dutoit—London LDR-71029)
Music of drama and lyrical warmth; good emotional / mental stimulus.

Larsson - Pastoral Suite (Westerberg—Swed. Soc.
SLT-33-176)
Nature oriented melodies paint tonal pictures of Scandinavian rural life;
kindles the imagination.

Lekeu - Violin Sonata (Philips 6500814)
Excellent for emotional / mental relaxation.

_____. Adagio for String Orchestra (DePriest—Radio
Canada International 454)
Very calming.

Liadov - Enchanted Lake (Szell—Epic BC 1272)
Mysterious and enchanting selection; promotes tranquility.

Lilburn, Douglas - Symphony No. 2 (Heenan—Kiwi SLD
48); Aotearoa Overture (Musical Heritage Soc. MHS-
3706A)
Magnificent music, majestic, lofty and powerfully dramatic; describes
nature in its pristine beauty and eruptive force and grandeur; a celebra-
tion of New Zealand's mountains and forests. The overture is celebrational, elicits courage, strength, and imagination / visualization.

Liszt - Battle of the Huns (Ansermet—London
STS-15475)
Dramatic, powerful cymbals and organ; good for release.

_____. Organ Transcriptions (Houbart—Harmonia
Mundi-HM 1-210)
Meditative and reflective; good for contemplation and spiritual center-
ing.

_____. Bells of Strassburg (Ferencsik—Hungaroton
SLPX-11797)
Dramatic and reverent music describing the overcoming of evil with the
power of Light; the chorus of the heavens mixes with cathedral bells;
good for encouragement.

_____. Christus (Forrai—Hungaroton
SLPX 11506-08)
Perhaps Liszt's greatest work: a mighty epic in music of the life of the
Christ from beginning to resurrection.

_____. Hungarian Rhapsodies (Dorati—Mercury 75018;
75089)
Beautifully colored and melodic dance music; wonderful for enlivening
body and emotions; good for relieving lethargy.

_____. Les Preludes (Fricsay—DGG 2535406)
Dramatic tone poem, at times highly energetic with great climaxes;
beautiful melodies; romantic sections.

MacDowell - To a Wild Rose (Ormandy—Columbia MS-7103)
Very pleasing; a natural for romance and reverie.

_____. Suite No. 2, Indian (Hanson—Mercury 75026)
Pictorial and dramatic; stimulates.

Mahler - Symphony No. 1, Titan (Walter—Odyssey Y-30047)
Marvelously poetic and dramatic; good for emotional release.

_____. Symphony No. 2, Resurrection (Baker, Bernstein—Columbia M2-32681)
Epic work: a tremendous statement of a spiritual seeker, culminating in drama of celestial choirs; a worship experience; good for spiritual inspiration.

_____. Symphony No. 3 (Bernstein—Columbia M2S-675)
Noble and inspirational work describing the journey of the composer and his interaction with nature; note the last movement which is especially suited for deep meditation.

_____. Symphony No. 9 (Walter—Odyssey Y-2-30308)
Total life statement; peaceful final movement.

Marcello - Recorder Sonatas (HNH-4086)
Transparent music that cleanses the atmosphere and emotions while uplifting the spirits.

Martini - Plaisir d'Amour (Sills, Kostelanetz—Columbia M-33933)
Beautiful song that awakens love.

Martinu - Symphony No. 6, Fantaisies symphoniques (Munch—RCA AGL1-3794)
A most dramatic symphony with many short, delightful moments of melody; depicts eventual resolution and surrender; good for pictorial imagination.

Massenet - Sleep of the Blessed Virgin (Frémaux—Klavier 522)
Peaceful and relaxing.

_____. Meditation, from Thais (Karajan—DGG 139031)
Linear; good for meditation and beautiful for listening.

McKuen, Rod - Concerto for Balloon (Stanyan—SR-9023)
A 20th century masterpiece: alternating dramatic segments with those that are meditative and floating; the finale which blends synthesizer and

organ is gorgeous; wonderful for imagination and deep reflection; joy-inspiring.

Mendelssohn - Violin Concerto (Campoli, Boult—London STS-15015)
Warm and mellow, calming and reassuring.

____. Elijah (Baker, Fruhbeck—Angel S-3738)
Inspiring, spiritual work, especially in its choral selections.

____. Symphony No. 4, Italian (Casals—Columbia MS-6931)
Refreshing, light and clearing.

Moeran - Symphony (Dilkes—EMI-ASD-2913)
Impassioned and beautiful.

Monteverdi - Vespers of the Blessed Virgin, 1610 (Schneidt—DGG ARC-2710017)
Excellent for awakening reverence and producing spiritual openings; meditative and healing.

Moreno Torroba - Iberian Concerto, guitar and orchestra (Romeros, Marriner—Philips 9500749)
Refreshing, clear and enlivening.

Mozart - Concertos for Flute (Rampal, Guschlbauer—RCA FRL 1-5330)
Both beautiful and refreshing.

____. Horn Concertos (Tuckwell, Marriner—Angel S-36840)
Energizing, joyful, clearing.

____. Ave Verum Corpus (Davis—Philips 6500271)
Beautiful and reverent; brings peace.

____. The Magic Flute (Bohm—DGG 2709017)
Based upon Masonic teachings; deeply esoteric and very inspiring description of man's spiritual quest.

____. A Little Night Music, Serenade in G (Walter—Odyssey Y30048)
Gorgeous, charming; refreshing to the spirit.

____. Piano Concertos (miscellaneous labels)
All beautiful, some very pensive and inspiring.

____. Koto Mozart (Angel S-37553)
Extremely different; a blending of Oriental sounds and Occidental melodies; very cleansing.

_____. Symphony No. 41, Jupiter (Odyssey Y-35493)
Powerful, joyous, exuberant.

_____. Posthorn Serenade (Szell—Columbia MS-7273)
Moving; sharp and cleansing.

Mundy - The Voice of the Heavenly Father (Classics for
Pleasure CFP-40339)
Inspiring and clear.

Mussorgsky - Night on Bald Mountain (Kletzki—London
STS-15530)
Pictorial and intriguing; explores the macabre versus transformation
and ends peacefully.

_____. Great Gate of Kiev, from Pictures at an Exhibition
(Leibowitz—Quintessence 7059; Toscanini—RCA
VIC-1273)
Inspires triumph and release into power; great theme, much drama.

Novák - About the Eternal Longing
(Sejna—Supraphon-50747)
Uplifting.

Orff - Carmina Burana (Blegen, Thomas—Columbia
33172)
Music with compelling drama and color; repetitions and montages of
sounds with strong rhythms; good for release / clearance.

Pachelbel - Canon in D (Paillard—Musical Heritage
1060Z)
Noble, gentling music; excellent for quieting nerves and for spiritual
devotion.

Palestrina - Pope Marcellus Mass (Willcocks—S-60187)
Serene, celestial, beautiful; good for intense meditation.

Parry, Sir Hubert - Symphony No. 5 (Boult—EMI-ASD
3725); I Was Glad (Guest—Polydor 2383-267); Jerusalem
(Polygram 6335); Blest Pair of Sirens (Boult—Vanguard
71225)
Stately, exquisite music.

Piston - The Incredible Flutist (Hanson—Mercury 75050)
Colorful and dramatic; brings cheer.

Ponchielli - Dance of the Hours, from La Gioconda
(Mackerras—Angel S-35833)
Stimulating; fast rhythms; quickens pulse.

Poulenc - Concerto for Organ, Timpani and Strings
(Pretre—Angel S-35953)
Powerful and dramatic, bringing strong energy and potential for release of anger; cathartic.

Prokofiev - Alexander Nevsky (Schippers—Odyssey
Y-31014)
Heroic music, mixing with some tragedy and battle scenes; galvanizing for the energy.

_____. Symphony No. 7 (Martinon—London STS-15195)
Some beautiful melodies here, and some sadness and nostalgic moments; I like the beauty of the themes and the stirring finale.

Purcell - Anthems (Preston—DGG ARC-2723076)
Majestic, devotional music; good for building faith and spiritual dedication.

Puccini - Greatest Hits (Kostelanetz—Columbia
16-11-0134)
Romantic and dramatic.

Rachmaninoff - Piano Concerto No. 2 (Ashkenazy,
Kondrashin—London 41001)
Dramatic music, building toward joyful overcoming in the finale which helped Rachmaninoff's own depression to lift.

_____. Piano Concerto No. 3 (Horowitz,
Ormandy—RCA CRL1-25333)
Highly charged, manic joy.

_____. Symphony No. 2 (Kletzki—London STS-15500;
Previn—Angel S-36954)
Spacious Russian canvas of drama, color and melody; the Adagio is particularly therapeutic and expansive.

_____. Rhapsody on a Theme of Paganini (Wild,
Horenstein—Quintessence 7006)
Many moments of power and rhythmic vitality; 18th variation is especially appealing; awakens love.

Rautavaara - Cantus Arcticus (Finlandia FA328)
A brooding, meditative piece, combining bird calls with orchestral colors; good for imagination and creativity.

Ravel - Piano Concerto for Left Hand (Browning,
Leinsdorf—Seraphim S-60224)
Perky and very strong in places; a total experience emotionally, exploring many feelings.

Respighi - Pines of Rome; Fountains of Rome (Kempe—
Quintessence 7005)
Some glorious color and varieties of sound here; the nightingale move-
ment is especially evocative and soothing.

____. Ancient Dances and Airs (Dorati—Mercury 75009)
Thoroughly enjoyable music filled with charm and changes of pace; a
therapeutic quality comes through its grace and vitality.

Rheinberger - Organ Concertos (Biggs, Peress—Columbia
M-32297)
Dramatic and powerful; good energizing music.

Rimsky-Korsakov - Scheherazade (Beecham—Angel
RL-32027; Haitink—Philips 6500410)
Has fairy tale quality; soars with melody and also with powerful drama;
good for pictorial creativity.

Rodrigo - Concierto de Aranjuez (P. Romero,
Marriner—Philips 9500563); Fantasy for a Courtier
(Biteti, Asencio—Turnabout 34636)
Lilting Spanish rhythms and tunes; middle movement of "Aranjuez"
particularly lovely and quieting.

Rossini - William Tell Overture; The Silken Ladder
(Abbado—DGG 2530559)
Alive, quickening; good for releasing tensions and anger.

Saint-Saens - Symphony No. 3, Organ (Zamkochian,
Munch—RCA ATL1-4039)
Electrifying piece, at times very quiet and reflective, but culminating in
grand finale, reminiscent of a cathedral rising stone by stone to the
heavens.

Schmidt, Franz - Intermezzo, from Notre Dame
(Karajan—DGG 139031)
Rising splendor; grand, expansive music of awe and joyous praise.

Schubert - Rosamunde, selections (Bohm—DGG 2530422)
Serene, joyous, reassuring.

____. Symphonies (various labels)
All bright and lyrical; "Unfinished" (Symphony No. 8) a bit more
somber; good for centering.

Schumann - Piano Concerto in A (Argerich,
Rostropovich—DGG 2531042); Symphony No. 1, 2
(Klemperer—Angel RL-32063); Träumerei, Dreams
(Ormandy—Columbia MS-6883)
Mostly dramatic and very inspiring; beautifully lyrical.

Sheriff - Essay for Harp and Strings (Mitchell—Argo
ZK92)
Refreshing.

Sibelius - Finlandia (Davis—Philips 9500140); Karelia
Suite (Ormandy—RCA ARL1-2613); Symphony No. 1,
2, 4, 6, 7 (Davis—Philips 9500140, 9500141, 9500142,
9500143, 6500959)
From the great master painter of nature music, compelling and surging
melodies; one needs concentrated reflection and immersion in order to
merge into the pieces.

Sinding - Symphony No. 2 (Ingebretsen—Norsk
Kulturrad NKF-30.011)
Wonderful Scandinavian qualities; expansive.

Smetana - My Country, Ma Vlast (Kubelik—DGG
2707054)
Epic qualities of ancient Bohemia; rich variety of emotions; wide range
of musical experience; powerful.

Sowande, Fela - African Suite (Freeman—Columbia
M-33433)
Appealing and melodic, especially the lullaby.

Sousa - Marches (Hunsberger—Philips 9500151)
Good energizers for body, encourage movement.

Strauss, Johann - Die Fledermaus Overture; Waltzes
(Dorati—London STS-15545; Reiner RCA-LSC2500)
Pleasing melodies, bringing uplift and joy; good for movement and
dancing.

Strauss, Richard - Aus Italien, From Italy
(Kempe—Seraphim S-60301); Also Sprach Zarathustra
(Reiner—RCA VICS-1265); Dance Suite after Couperin
(Rodzinski—Seraphim S-60030); Don Juan (Bohm—DGG
2535208); Death and Transfiguration (Reiner—RCA
VICS-1004)
Highly varied music: some really dramatic (i.e. "Sunrise" from *Also
Sprach Zarathustra*) and the ethereal beauty of the "Death and
Transfiguration" finale which brings in angelic harmonies.

Stravinsky - Firebird (Stokowski—London 212026)
Exotic, stimulating, powerful release music.

Sullivan - Irish Symphony (Groves—EMI-ASD-2435)
Beautiful and exhilarating.

Sumac - Chants of the Incans (Capitol SM-684)
Exotic and haunting.

Suppe - Poet and Peasant Overture; Light Cavalry
Overture (Bernstein—Columbia D3S-318)
Very stimulating; good to relieve lethargy or the doldrums.

Tallis - Spem in alium, 40-part motet (Willcocks—Argo
ZRG-5436)
Celestial; uplifting, devotional music.

Tchaikovsky - Capriccio Italien (Barenboim—DGG
2532022); Piano Concertos No. 1, 2 (Graffman,
Szell—Columbia MS-7339; Ormandy—Columbia
MS-6755); Symphony No. 1, Winter Dreams
(Thomas—DGG 2530078); Symphony No. 5
(Monteux—RCA AGL1-1264); 1812 Overture
(Sharples—London 21001); Romeo and Juliet
(Abbado—DGG 2530137); Swan Lake (Rowicki—DGG
2535371)
Combination of martial rhythms, colorful melodies, and great emo-
tional swings: some of the music very manic, other parts calm and
reflective.

Telemann - Table Music (Wenzinger—DGG Archive
2723-074-10)
Lively and stimulating.

Thompson, Randall - Suite for Oboe, Clarinet and Viola
(Crystal S-321)
Calming and strengthening.

Thomson, Virgil - The River (Stokowski—Vanguard
2095)
Americana at its finest: beautiful scenic music, great for imagination.

Vaughan Williams - Fantasia on a Theme of Thomas
Tallis (Stokowski—Desmar 1011G); Job (Boult—Angel
S-36773); Lark Ascending (Bean, Boult—Angel S-36902);
selections from his nine symphonies, especially Nos. 1, 2,
3, 5 (Previn—RCA, various discs); Oxford Elegy (Angel
S-36699)
Music of nobility with pastoral / dramatic / folksong ingredients;
restores sense of order and rightness; splendid listening, often highly
charged.

Verdi - Choruses (miscellaneous labels)
Energizing.

Vivaldi - Four Seasons (Galway—RCA LLR1-2284);
Guitar Concerto in D (Yepes—London CS 6201); Flute

Concertos (Rampal—Columbia D3S-770); Sacred Music
(Negri—Philips, various discs); Gloria (Willcocks—Argo-
ZRG-505); Organ Concertos (Isoir, Kuentz—DGG
2530652)

Very therapeutic music; alive and light; good for cleansing; releases staleness.

Wagner - Die Meistersinger Overture and Prelude;
Parsifal, Prelude and Good Friday Music; Lohengrin,
Prelude to Act 1; Flying Dutchman Overture (for all
selections: look for Furtwangler, Walter and Klemperer
renditions for depth; Stokowski's versions for color and
grandeur—various labels)

Powerful, demanding music; high voltage works which are uplifting and expansive; *Parsifal* is good for spiritual deepening and devotion.

Weber - Symphonies Nos. 1 and 2 (Schönzler—RCA VIC
CRL2-2281); Overtures (Bernstein—Columbia M-33585)

Very stirring and activating music.

Yardumian - Song of the Soul and Heart
(Brusilow—HNH-4043)

Gorgeous!

2. LIGHTER SELECTIONS

Adoro - Domingo (Columbia FM-37284)

Some beautiful love songs for tenor and orchestra.

Ancient Shepherd Pipes (Hillel—Folkways-FW-8724)

Haunting and lovely.

Anderson, Hans Christian (Danny Kaye, Jenkins—
MCA 148)

Friendly music and good story for children and adults.

Anderson, Marian - Spirituals (RCA-AVM1-1735)

Very therapeutic; beautiful singing; deep, devotional experience.

Avenging and Bright (Charles Guard, Celtic
harp—Shanachie 79014)

Lively and energizing music; good for relieving lethargy.

Beauty of Maori Song (Kiwi SLC-122)

Soulful songs and chants from New Zealand, often with mantra-like qualities; some songs very activating, others meditative.

Best Years of Our Lives (Entr'acte-8101)
Exhilarating.

Bernstein, Elmer - Themes from General Electric Theatre
(Columbia ACS-8190)
Some beautiful melodies here; at times quiet, but mostly energizing.

Bok, Gordon - Peter Kagan and the Wind; Bay of Fundy;
Sea Djiril's Hymn (Folk Legacy FSI 44; FSI 54; FSI 48)
Soothing voice; music that calms.

Born Free, soundtrack (MGM-4368-ST)
Beautiful and stirring; African rhythms provide means for greater mental focus.

Brother Sun, Sister Moon, soundtrack (Paramount
CO 64-93393)
Exquisite soundtrack music, some vocal (in Italian), some instrumental, suggesting the life of St. Francis of Assisi.

Carolan's Receipt (Derek Bell, Irish
Harp—Shanachie-79013)
Lively and cheerful sounds.

Collins, Judy - Colors of the Day (Elektra TC-55030)
Melodic love songs and ballads; pleasing instrumental accompaniment; mellow; stirs imagination.

Caravans, soundtrack (Epic-35787)
Exotic film score containing centering rhythms and melodies; exceptionally energizing and at times nostalgic.

Chants of Yogananda (Haridas, piano—Living Joy, 14618
Tyler Foote Rd., Nevada City, CA 95959)
Reverent, joyful music of praise and devotion.

Chariots of Fire, soundtrack (Polydor-6335)
Very powerful music; fine for indecision and lethargy treatment.

Nat King Cole - Stardust; When the World Was Young
(K-tel-PTP-2058-A)
Extremely relaxing, nostalgic; good for relieving tensions.

Denver, Domingo - Perhaps Love (CBS-37243); Seasons
of the Heart, Denver only (RCA AFL1-4256)
Some really lovely music here; melodic, inspiring and with uplifting words; good for relieving depression and self-pity.

Dexter - Golden Voyage I, III, IV (Awakening Productions, Culver City, CA)

Music that cleanses the aura; purifying and elevating / relaxing; synthesizers, nature sounds, etc.

Dr. Zhivago, soundtrack (MGM 1SE-6)
Contains famous "Lara's Theme" and much inspiring music.

Danny Boy (White, Gerhardt—RCA ARL1-3442)
Irish ballads, some enlivening, others exploring melancholy and nostalgia.

Diamond, Neil - Jonathan Livington Seagull (Columbia JS-32550)
Haunting music that both inspires and captivates; in some places very soft, in others strong.

The Empire Strikes Back, soundtrack (RSO 2-4201)
Strong music that energizes the system.

E.T., soundtrack (MCA-6109)
Music that alternates between mystery and forcefulness; good for inspiration in the more dynamic places.

Environments - Psychologically Ultimate Seashore, Optimum Aviary (Syntonic Research SD-66001)
Soothing sounds; good for deep meditation.

Echoes of a Waterfall (Drake—Hyperion A-66038)
Romantic harp music of the 19th century; transparent; provides openings; energizing and relaxing.

Evening Bells (Gedda—Seraphim S-60225)
Glorious Russian sounds of balalaika and folksongs.

Fiedler, Arthur - Those Were the Days (RCA LSC-3261)
Nostalgic songs of yesteryear; good spirit; inspiring.

Flagstad, Kirsten - Great Sacred Songs (London OS-25038)
Inspiring, devotional hymns and anthems, especially Parry's "Jerusalem."

Flowers from the Silence - (David and Amanda Hughes—Vedic Research Institute, 415 S. Bernardo, Sunnyvale, CA 94068)
Quiet music; Oriental flavor, at times a bit austere, yet compelling and meditative; nature sounds and various contemporary sounds.

Floating Petals...Wild Geese...The Moon on High, music for Chinese pipa (Nonesuch H-72085)
Enlivening, clear, hauntingly joyful and accepting.

For a Child's Heart (Synergetic Media, SMC-7801)
Beautiful songs for children; joyous and very devotional.

Fox, Virgil - Heavy Organ at Carnegie Hall (RCA
    ARD1-0081)
Powerful organ music of Bach, energizing and enlivening.

Fiddler on the Roof, soundtrack (RCA LSO-1093)
Some festive music, basically energizing.

Galway, James - Song of the Seashore (RCA
    ARL1-3534); The Long White Cloud and Waiata Poi
    (RCA-AFL1-4063)
Flute music of the Orient and New Zealand—poetic, nostalgic, tender.

Garfunkel - Angel Clare (Columbia KC-31474)
I especially like the rendition of "Barbara Allen" which is very caressing
and warm.

Gibson, Dan - Solitudes (Dan Gibson Prod., Box 1200,
    Station Z, Toronto, Ontario M5N 2Z7, Canada)
Extremely therapeutic musical sounds of nature, including gentle
streams, gurgling brooks, heavy and light surf, sounds of the prairie,
redwood forests, etc. This music is also good for reverie and relaxing to
the body (six volumes).

Glorious (Abraham Kaplan—North American Liturgy
    Resources, Phoenix, AZ 85029)
Celebrational psalms.

The Good, the Bad and the Ugly, soundtrack (Liberty
    L0-05172)
Haunting and evocative music suggesting feelings of the West, the
desert, and the echoes off canyon walls; good for emotional release.

DeHartmann - Journey to Inaccessible Places (P.O. Box
    5961, Grand Central Station, New York, NY 10163)
Mysterious music, often hypnotic in its rhythms and suggestive of inner
landscapes.

Hoffmann - Music for the Glass Harmonica (Philips
    9500397)
Exotic sounds that suggest both antiquity and timelessness.

Horn, Paul - Inside the Taj Mahal (Epic BXN-26466)
Marvelously meditative music; some for solo flute has the floating ambience that takes the listener upward in consciousness.

Hymns Triumphant (Holdridge, arranger—Birdwing
    BWC-2023)

Beautiful and devotional arrangements; many great hymns; powerful choral singing; good for upliftment and reverence.

The Incas (Philips 6620-040)
Music of South America; festive, strong rhythms; powerful; very melodic and energizing.

Iasos - Angels of Comfort (Inter-Dimensional Music, Box 594, Sausalito, CA 94965)
Floating music for synthesizer; lifting music that goes nowhere but is here now; makes no demands upon the listener; suggests peacefulness.

Ice Flowers Melting - Finnish Folk Harp (Fortuna Records, 11 Kavon Ct., Novato, CA 94947)
Crystalline sounds creating feelings of transparency and cleansing.

Javanese Court Gamelan (Nonesuch H-72074)
Exotic sounds of gongs and Balinese music that is both praise-filled and worshipful; stimulates the system.

Jackson, Mahalia - Hymns (Folkways FTS-31102)
Music of praise; reveals a large, loving heart; deeply devotional.

Kelly-Halpern - Ancient Echoes (SRI-783-H)
Music that calms and centers; good for relieving hyperactivity. I personally like the non-chanting, purely instrumental harp music best.

Kennedy, Calum - Scottish Songs (Golden Hour GH593)
Music filled with energy and warmth; promotes warmth and friendliness.

Kleinsinger - Tubby the Tuba (Jenkins—MCA-148)
Story and music combine to bring joy and good humor; uplifting.

Lanza - I'll Walk with God (RCA-LSC-2607 E)
A voice filled with ardor and devotion; music that inspires and uplifts.

Liberace - The Best of Liberace (Decca 73-7209)
Music of exuberance, flare and good spirit.

Lee, Jonathan - In His Loving (J. Lee, 1136 2nd St., Suite 4, Encinitas, CA 92024)
I have heard Mr. Lee sing songs of spiritual devotion; there is warmth and generosity in his voice.

Lee, Gabriel - Oriental Sunrise (Celestial Spaces - Plumeria, Box 54, Kailus, HI 96734)
Music for koto; meditative, relaxing, expansive; good for hyperactivity release.

Lutunn Noz - Celtic Music for Guitar (Musical Heritage Society 5577)

Marvelously uplifting music, good for release of tightness; also good for relieving boredom.

Lyre Bird (Concorde, Hastings, New Zealand JD202)
The songs of the lyre brid are evocative and exotic; many different songs here, of different moods and colors; I find this music most stimulating and helpful for lethargy.

Malotte - The Lord's Prayer (Mormon Tabernacle Choir—Columbia MS-6367)
Music that ennobles and uplifts; good for deepening devotion and dedication to God and Christ.

Mantovani - Miscellaneous albums, particularly Evening Star (London 921)
Pleasant, reassuring music; quite linear in places, thus building stability.

Misa Criolla (Philips Sequenza 6527136); Misa Luba (Philips Sequenza 6527137)
Modern settings of the Mass, bringing out exotic flavors and energizing rhythms.

McDonald, Susann - World of the Harp (Delos-DMS-3005)
Magnificent for clearance; the harp sounds and the melodies played here help one to ventilate immediately.

Montoya, Carlos - Malagueña (RCA AFL-12380)
Compelling guitar music, alternating between reflective and introspective and strong, earthy rhythms; good for clearing out the system.

Morgan, Melissa - Music to Sooth and Relax, solo harp (Box 4024, San Diego, CA 92104)
Music of varying moods, sometimes more forceful, other times more spatial and non-directed; in general, it defuses pressures and tensions.

Murooka - Lullaby from the Womb (Capitol ST-11421)
Music to help the birthing process; Dr. Murooka suggests good music for pregnancy and also includes the sound of a mother's heartbeat along with the music.

Music for Mandolin and Guitar Ensemble (Hladky—Vox CT-2266)
Both pleasant and percussive; good for energizing.

Music for Zen Meditation (Verve 16-8634)
Mysteriously unfolding, like flower petals.

National Anthems of the World, especially Star-Spangled Banner (Everest 3329)

Powerful melodies and stirring rhythms; good for overcoming lethargy and boredom.

New Troubadours - Winds of Birth (Lorian Assoc., Box
1095, Elgin, IL 60120)

Songs of the new Aquarian planetary age of brotherhood, cooperation and joyfulness in the Spirit; cuts across barriers of rigidity and blockage.

Norman, Jessye - Sacred Songs (Philips 6514151)

Powerful, devotional music; I especially like the consciousness-raising rendition of "Sanctus" by Gounod.

Nun's Story, soundtrack (Stanyan-4022)

Dramatic and reflective music.

Our Wedding (101 Strings—Alshire ALSC-5284)

Music for more traditional weddings, but most pleasingly performed.

Ortmans, Kay - Deep Relaxation (Wellsprings, 11667
Alba Rd., Ben Lomond, CA 95005)

Spoken and music. Pleasing rhythms to help listener air out anxiety and tension. Other tapes of music in this series are good for movement and body work.

Oklahoma, soundtrack (Columbia OS-2610)

Marvelous, perky tunes and energizing music.

Pavarotti - O Sole Mio, Neapolitan Songs (London
26560)

Powerful and passionate songs of love, friendship and reflection; brings out heart chakra energy.

Paco de Lucia - Master of the Spanish Guitar (Philips
6695001)

Music of power and songfulness; explores many different emotions; good for reverie and clearance.

Partita Teresiana (DiVietri, guitar solo—Teresian
Records, Box 2525, San Rafael, CA 94912)

Music recorded in a monastery; has reverent, devotional beauty to it; melodies that soar and an uplifting quality of spirit.

Phases of the Moon (CBS M-36705)

Traditional Chinese music of nature and exotic beauty that is also simple and appealing in its folksong style; good for energizing and, in some places, for reflection.

Psalms of David (Willcocks—EMI-TC-CSD-3656)

Deeply mantra-like in their repeated cadences, these melodies of devotion get inside the listener in a cleansing way.

Peerce, Jan — Bluebird of Happiness (RCA-VIC-1553)
Moving solos of melodic and emotional depth; Peerce's voice has power and tonal richness; arouses deep feelings.

Parkening, Christopher - Bach (Angel S-36041)
All the great Bach favorites, played on a clear-sounding guitar; this music is healing and quieting, getting inside the listener and bringing cleansing.

Rodgers, Richard - Victory at Sea (Gerhardt—
Quintessence PMC 7032)
Strong, powerfully compelling music; breaks up blockage.

Roth - You Are the Ocean (Heavenly Music, Box 1063,
Larkspur, CA 94939)
Very pleasing and low-keyed in its approach; expansive melodies; excellent for relieving tension in a quiet way.

Rosewood and Silver, guitar and flute (Nimbus Music,
Box 10321, Bainbridge Island, WA 98110)
Several classics arranged for guitar and flute make this a beautiful listening experience. The pieces are mostly quieting and melodically pleasing.

Rampal, Jean Pierre - Miscellaneous albums
You cannot go wrong buying Rampal's tasteful, elegant expressions of music. The flute sounds help to unwind the emotions and they clear out the system.

Recorder Concertos (Petri, Brown—Philips-7300808)
Eloquent and cleansing.

Stivell - Renaissance of the Celtic Harp (Polydor
2424-069)
Deeply soulful experiences in this music of ocean waves and haunting melodies played on the Celtic harp. Good for reverie and introspection.

Somewhere in Time, soundtrack (MCA-5154)
Ultimately satisfying; deeply romantic, expansive, warm music; includes Rachmaninoff's 18th variation from *Rhapsody on a Theme of Paganini*; music that awakens deep soul memories and loving emotions.

Sound of Music, soundtrack (RCA LSOD-2005)
One of the greatest pieces of music ever composed; the "Prologue," "Climb Every Mountain," and "Edelweiss" are especially therapeutic and should be played in sequence if possible; brings in the joy of the angels and the strong currents of encouragement.

Spirit Alive (Monks of the Western Priory, Weston, VT
05161)

Contemporary songs of joy and the Christian spirit; these songs are simple statements of wellsprings of devotion, excellent for sing-along, either by oneself or in groups of friends.

Standin' Tall (Granere, 330 Avenida Chapala, San Marcos, CA 92069)
Wonderful for children.

Star Wars, soundtrack (Warner Brothers 2BSK-3257)
Bold, energetic score replete with suspense and involvement; excellent for tiredness or mild depression.

Sufi Choir Sings Kabir (Shyne Sound, San Rafael, CA)
Somewhat Oriental in flavor yet accessible to the Western ear; I like the devotional quality of the music; many beautiful melodies.

Superman, soundtrack (Warner Brothers 2BSK-3257)
Strong, enlivening music; filled with drama and excitement; good for combating lethargy and the "blahs."

Talbot, John Michael - Come to the Quiet (Birdwing BWR-2019)
Contemporary monk-like songs of devotion; a strong feeling of solitude and contemplation accompanies the music; good for spiritual aspiration.

Tibetan Bells - I (Antilles AN-7006); II (Pacific Arts Records PACR7-110)
Music for strong focus and mental centering; deep resonances and cosmic expanse of gong-like sounds.

Theodorakis - Music for Bouzouki and Orchestra (Galata Gal-503)
Very stimulating Greek rhythms; arouse desires to dance; good for lifting one out of introversion.

Ten Commandments, soundtrack (Paramount 1006)
Epic music, strong and demanding: some memorable melodies and strong rhythms.

Tremolo (Teña, Ramos—Musical Heritage 972)
Music of Spain, intoxicating with its rhythms and melodies, highlighted by Teña's castanets.

Vanity Fair (Neel—Citadel Records CT-6013)
The pleasing little melody "Vanity Fair" by Anthony Collins is especially charming in its direct appeal.

Winter, Paul - Callings (Living Music Records, Box 68, Litchfield, CT 06759)

Music that combines instruments and nature calls of animals and ocean; I do not like the "jazzy" sections, but mostly this is very ennobling music that deepens one's appreciation of and affiliation with nature.

When You Wish Upon A Star (CBS-37200)
Walt Disney Songs; marvelously uplifting.

Whistle While You Work (Mormon Tabernacle Choir—CBS M-35868)
A marvelous pick-up for early morning; tones the day ahead with joy and focus.

Windwalker, soundtrack (Jenson—Cerberus Records, CST-0202)
Marvelous music of the West, combining melodies and instrumental sounds that bring to mind Paul Horn's "Inside the Taj Mahal" and other exotic flute melodies; good for reflection and some stirring up.

Yellow River Concerto (Ormandy—RCA-ARL-1-0415)
Beautiful Oriental melodies.

You Light Up My Life (Debby Boone—Warner Brothers BS-3118)
Sparkling and uplifting love song; very romantic and inspiring; expresses intimacy and caring.

Zamfir, Music for flute of Pan (various albums on miscellaneous labels, especially Mercury and Philips.)
Exotic sound of the Pan flute make this music excellent for defusing from busyness; also good for creative imagination.

3. CHRISTMAS MUSIC

Bach Choir Family Carols (Willcocks—London-LDR5-10028)

Bach, J. S. - The Christmas Oratorio (Thomas—Seraphim S-6040)

Baez - Noël (Vanguard VRS-9230)

Belafonte - To Wish You a Merry Christmas (RCA LPM-1887)

Berlioz - L'Enfance du Christ (Martinon—Nonesuch H-73022)

Casals - El Pesebre, The Manger (Casals—Columbia M2-32966)

Chadwick - Noël, from Symphonic Sketches (Hanson—Mercury 75050)

Charpentier - Pastoral for the Birth of Jesus Christ (Harmonia Mundi HM-1082)

Christmas Eve at the Cathedral of St. John the Divine (Westenburg—Vanguard VSD-71212)

Christmas Music from Kings (Willcocks—EMI HMV-ESD-7050)

Christmas Songs from Europe (Ameling—Peters PLE-092)

Christmas with the New York Harp Ensemble (von Wurtzler—Musical Heritage MHS--5483)

Dragon - Lullaby of Christmas (Peck—Decca DL-78009)

The Glorious Sound of Christmas (Ormandy—Columbia MS-6369)

Handel - Messiah (Willcocks—Arabesque 8030)

Holst - Ceremony of Carols (Willcocks—Seraphim-S-60217)

_____. A Dream of Christmas (Aston—University of East Anglia-NR4-7TJ)

Ives - A Christmas Carol (Western Wind—Musical Heritage-4077A)

The Joy of Christmas (Crystal Cathedral: Rev. Robert Schuller—RFJ-8101)

Mormon Tabernacle Choir Sings Christmas Carols (Condie—Columbia MS-6777)

On Christmas Night (Willcocks—Argo ZRG-5333)

Once in Royal David's City (Willcocks—EMI-CSD-3698)

Parry - Ode on the Nativity (Willcocks—Lyrita-SRCS-125)

Pavarotti - O Holy Night (London OS5-26473)

Price, Leontyne - A Christmas Offering (London OS5-25280)

Respighi - Adoration of the Magi, from Botticellian Triptych (Heltay—Argo ZRG-904)

Rosenberg - Holy Night (Ericson—SR Records RELP-5007)

Vaughan Williams - Hodie (Willcocks—Angel S-36297); The Sons of Light (Willcocks—Lyrita SRCS-125)

4. AN EASTER PROGRAM

J. S. Bach - Come Sweet Death, organ solo

_____. Jesu, Joy of Man's Desiring (Flagstad)

> Jesu, joy of man's desiring,
> Holy wisdom, love most bright:
> Drawn by Thee, our souls aspiring
> Soar to uncreated Light.
> Word of God, our flesh that fashioned,
> With the fire of Light impassioned,
> Striving still to truth unknown,
> Soaring, dying round Thy throne;
> Through the way where hope is guiding,
> Hark what peaceful music rings,
> Where the flock in Thee confiding
> Drink of joy in deathless springs.
> Theirs is beauty's fairest pleasure,
> Theirs is wisdom's holiest treasure.
> Thou dost ever lead Thine own
> In the love of joys unknown.
>
>   Text by Robert Bridges

Ludwig van Beethoven - Hallelujah, from Christ on the Mount of Olives

> Hallelujah, Hallelujah, Hallelujah, Hallelujah,
> Unto God's Almighty Son!
> Praise the Lord, ye bright angelic choirs, in holy songs of joy.
> Praise the Lord in holy, holy songs of joy.
> Man, proclaim His grace and glory.
> Hallelujah, Hallelujah, Hallelujah, Hallelujah,
> Unto God's Almighty Son.
> Praise the Lord, praise the Lord,
> In Holy songs of joy.

Gabriel Fauré - In Prayer

> If the voice of a child can reach you,
> Listen, O my Father, to the prayer of Jesus Christ
>   kneeling before you;
> If you have chosen me to teach your laws on earth,
> I shall know how to serve you, King of Kings, O Light.
> Place on my lips the solitary truth,
> That he who doubts reveres you with humility.

Do not abandon me, Give me the sweetness needed to
   cure the ills;
Relieve the pain and misery;
Reveal yourself to me, in whom I place my faith and
   hope.

Charles Gounod - Sanctus, from St. Cecilia Mass

_____. Unfold Ye Portals, from Redemption

Unfold! Unfold! Unfold! Ye portals everlasting!
With welcome to receive Him ascending on High.
Behold the King of Glory!
He mounts up through the sky
Back to heavenly mansions hasting,
Unfold - Unfold, for lo, the King comes nigh.

But who is He the King of Glory?
He who Death overcame, the Lord in battle mighty.
But who is He, the King of Glory?
Of hosts He is the Lord, of angels and of powers;
The King of Glory is the King of Saints.

George Frideric Handel - Hallelujah Chorus, from Messiah

Franz Liszt - Resurrexit, He Is Risen, from Christus

Gustav Mahler - Finale from Symphony No. 2, Resurrection

With wings that I have won
in fervent, loving aspiration,
will I soar to the Light
that no eye has ever seen.
I shall die that I may live.

Richard Wagner - Prelude to Act 1 of Lohengrin, music of the
   Holy Grail and the descent of angels from on High

Hugo Wolf - Night Is Almost Ended

Night is almost ended,
Already I feel morning breezes blowing.
The Lord who says: "Let there be Light."
Then all the darkness must vanish.
From the vault of Heaven, throughout the whole world
The rejoicing Angels fly:
The sun's rays light up the universe.
Lord, let us fight, let us win.

Other Recommended Listening at Easter
(Found on Various Labels)

J. S. Bach - St. Matthew Passion; St. John Passion; Easter Oratorio

Anton Bruckner - Adagio from Symphony No. 7; Adagio from Symphony No. 8

Paul Creston - Symphony No. 3, third movement: Resurrection

Sir Edward Elgar - The Apostles

Joseph Foerster - Symphony No. 4: Easter

César Franck - Beatitudes; Redemption; Panis Angelicus

Franz Joseph Haydn - The Seven Last Words of Christ

Alan Hovhaness - Magnificat

Giovanni Pergolesi - Stabat Mater

Randall Thompson - Alleluia

Antonio Vivaldi - Kyrie; Gloria

Richard Wagner - Prelude and Good Friday Music, from Parsifal

5. MUSIC OF NATURE AND THE SEASONS

Miscellaneous

The Ancient Shepherd Pipes, Israeli (Folkways FW 8724)

A Bell Ringing in an Empty Sky, Japanese (Nonesuch-H72025)

Gluck, Christoph Willibald - Dance of the Blessed Spirits (Seraphim S-60278)

Peach Blossom Time, Chinese (The Cowherds—Candide CE 31037)

Respighi - Pines of Rome; Fountains of Rome (London 21024)

Song of the Seashore, Japanese (Galway, flute—RCA ARL1-3534)

Sowande, Fela - African Suite (Ace of Diamonds SDD 2214)

The Four Seasons

Carlos - Sonic Seasonings (Columbia PG-31234)

Glazunov - The Seasons (London 6509)

Tchaikovsky - The Seasons (Columbia/Melodiya MG-35184)

Verdi - The Four Seasons (Angel SZ-37801)

Vivaldi - The Four Seasons (RCA LRL 1-2284; Philips 6500017)

Spring

Beethoven - Spring Sonata, Sonata No. 5 in F for Violin and Piano (DGG 2531300)

Britten - Spring Symphony (Angel S-37562)

Delius - On Hearing the First Cuckoo in Spring (Seraphim S-60185)

Eto, Kimio - Bright Morning, koto (World Pacific Records, rare)

Hadley - The Hills (EMI-Odeon SAN 393)

Iasos - Essence of Spring, including brook and bird songs (Inter-dimensional Music, Sausalito, CA)

Miyagi - The Sea of the Spring (Columbia CS 9381, rare)

Respighi - Spring, from Botticellian Triptych (Argo ZRG 904)

Schumann - Symphony No. 1, Spring (Angel RL-32063)

Sinding - Rustle of Spring (Klavier KF-111)

Stravinsky - Rite of Spring (London STS-15318)

Strauss, Johann - Voices of Spring (RCA LSC 5005)

Summer

Beethoven - Symphony No. 6, Pastorale (RCA LSC-2614; Angel S-35711)

Brahms - Symphony No. 2 (Philips Festivo 6570108)

Debussy - Printemps; The Sea (RCA VICS-1041, Columbia MS-7361)

Delius - Florida Suite; A Song of Summer; Summer Night on the River; In a Summer Garden (Seraphim S-60212)

D'Indy - Symphony on a French Mountain Air (Odyssey Y-31274)

Dvořák - Silent Woods (Angel S-36046)

Honegger - Summer Pastorale (Columbia-MS-6659)

Hovhaness - Mysterious Mountain (RCA AGL-1-4215)

Kodaly - Summer Evening (London 6864)

Rimsky-Korsakov - May Night (Turnabout 34689)

Schoeck - Summer Night (Genesis 1010)

Sibelius - Symphony No. 6 (Philips 95000143)

Song of the Seashore (Galway—RCA ARL 1-3534)

Vaughan Williams - Symphony No. 3, Pastoral (Angel S-36532)

Autumn

Grieg - Nocturne, from Lyric Suite (Seraphim S-60032)

Ives - The Pond (CRI 163)

MacDowell - Autumn Leaves (Philips 9500095)

Porter - New England Episodes (Desto 7123)

Prokofiev - Autumn (London 7063)

Strauss, R. - From Italy (Seraphim S-60301)

Thomson, V. - Autumn (Angel S-37300)

Vaughan Williams - In the Fen Country (Angel S-36532); Lark Ascending (Angel S-36902)

Winter

Grieg - Piano Concerto (London STS-15407; Quintessence 7031)

Sibelius - Symphony No. 4 (Philips 95000142); The Tempest (Columbia-30390)

Strauss, R. - An Alpine Symphony (London 7189)

Tchaikovsky - Symphony No. 1, Winter Dreams (DGG 2530078)

Vaughan Williams - Symphony No. 7, Antarctica (Angel S-36763)

6. ADDITIONAL CHILDREN'S MUSIC

Pre-Natal and Infancy

"In the germ, when the first trace of life begins to stir, music is the nurse of the Soul; it murmurs in the ear, and the child sleeps; the tones are companions of his dreams—they are the world in which he lives." (Bettini)

Bach, J. S. - Two Flute Concertos (James Galway—RCA ARK1-2907)

Barry, John - Somewhere in Time, soundtrack (MCA 5154)

Brahms - Lullaby (Columbia M-30307)

Debussy - Clair de lune (Columbia MS-6884)

Dexter, Ron - Golden Voyage I, III, IV (Awakening Productions, Culver City, CA)

Humperdinck - Children's Prayer (Columbia MS 6884)

Koto Flute (Ransom Wilson, flute, and koto orchestra—Angel 4XS-37325)

Mozart - Piano Concerto No. 21, slow movement (Columbia MT-34562)

Pachelbel - Canon in D (Musical Heritage Society MHS 2060)

Roth - You Are the Ocean (Heavenly Music, Box 1063, Larkspur, CA 94939)

The Story of Celeste (Cricket Records CR-16)

World of the Harp (Susann McDonald-Delos DMS-3005-D)

Ages 3-5

Play melodious music with clear rhythms but nothing heavy or raucous. Encourage your children to make and play their own instruments; teach them rhythms and open them to the mysteries of sounds. Avoid rock beat!

Bizet - Symphony No. 1 and Children's Games (DGG-3335238)

Copland - Lincoln Portrait (Vanguard S-348); Old American Songs (Columbia MS-6497)

Delibes - Coppelia (Columbia MT-31845)

Golden Slumbers, lullabies (Caedmon TC-1399)

Harsanyi - The Story of the Little Tailor (Angel S-36357)

Haydn - Symphony No. 45; Toy Symphony; Trumpet Concerto (Seraphim S-60294)

Mendelssohn - Overture and Selections from A Midsummer Night's Dream (London STS-15084)

Music for Recorder (Kosofsky—Titanic 7)
Prokofiev - Peter and the Wolf (Angel 4XS-36644)
Rimsky-Korsakov - Scheherazade (Columbia MS-7509)
Rossini - Overtures (Seraphim 4XG-60282)
Snow White and the Seven Dwarfs (Disneyland Records)
Sousa - Marches (London 139)
Strauss, Johann - Blue Danube Waltz and other Strauss waltzes
    (Columbia D3S-789)
Villa-Lobos - Little Train of the Caipira (Everest 3041)
Weber - Overtures (DGG-3300294)
When You Wish Upon a Star (CBS-37200)

Ages 6-12

Introduce your children to music of many lands and to the beauty
of the orchestra.

The Black Stallion, soundtrack (Liberty L00-01040)
Britten - Young Person's Guide to the Orchestra, coupled with
    Saint Saens' Carnival of the Animals (Columbia MT-31808)
Diamond, Neil - Jonathan Livingston Seagull (Diamond—Colum-
    bia KS-32550)
James, Terry - Jonathan Livingston Seagull (Richard
    Harris—ABC-DSD-50160)
Mozart - Symphony No. 41, Jupiter (DGG 3335114)
The Nonesuch Explorer Series of Music from All Over the World
    (Nonesuch Records)
Seraphim Guide to the Instruments of the Orchestra (Seraphim
    S-60234)
Tchaikovsky - 1812 Overture (London 21001)
Three Cheers for Pooh (Musical Heritage Soc. MHS 4617)
Zamfir, music for flute of Pan (various albums on miscellaneous
    labels, especially Mercury and Philips)

Miscellaneous

Ann Rachlin - Fun with Music, Volumes 1-20 (EMI, England)
    Beautiful stories plus classical music background, perfectly
    woven into the story line.
Valerie Dunbar - Scottish Lovesongs
Velveteen Rabbit (Windham Hill)

Bibliography

FOR FURTHER STUDY AND READING

Abell, Arthur. *Talks With The Great Composers*. Verlag, Germany: G. E. Schroeder, 1964.

Alberti, Luciano. *Music of the Western World*. New York: Crown Publ., 1968.

Andrews, Donald Hatch. *The Symphony of Life*. Lee's Summit, MO: Unity Books, 1966.

Assagioli, Roberto. *Psychosynthesis*. New York: Viking Compass, 1965.

Baker, Richard. *The Magic of Music*. New York: Universe Books, 1975.

Benjamin, Edward B. *The Restful in Music*. Boston: Crescendo Publishing Co., 1964.

Bonny, Helen. *Music and Your Mind*. New York: Harper & Row, 1973.

Cayce, Edgar. *Music As the Bridge*. Virginia Beach: A.R.E. Press, 1972.

Commins, Dorothy. *All About the Symphony Orchestra*. New York: Random House, 1961.

Cousins, Norman. *The Anatomy of an Illness*. New York: Norton Publ., 1979.

Cross, Milton & Ewen, David. *Encyclopedia of Great Composers and Their Music*. Garden City, NY: Doubleday, 1962.

Diamond, John. *BK, Behavioral Kinesiology*. New York: Harper & Row, 1979. (Published in paperback with title *Your Body Doesn't Lie*. New York: Warner Books, Inc., 1980.)

———. *The Life Energy in Music*. Valley Cottage, N.Y.: Archaens Press, 1981.

Einstein, Alfred. *Greatness in Music*. New York: Oxford University Press, 1941.

Gal, Hans, (ed.). *The Musician's World*. New York: Arco Publ., 1966.

Gammond, Peter. *The Meaning and Magic of Music*. New York: Golden Press, 1970.

Gilder, Eric, & Port, June. *Dictionary of Composers and Their Music*. New York: Ballantine, 1978.

Gutheil, Emil. *Music and Your Emotions.* New York: Liveright, 1952.

Hall, Manly P. *Music Through the Ages* (a talk). Los Angeles: The Philosophical Reseach Society, 1972.

Headington, Christopher. *The Orchestra and Its Instruments.* Cleveland: World Publ. Co., 1965.

Heline, Corinne. *Beethoven's Nine Symphonies.* Santa Barbara: J. F. Rowny Press, 1965.

_____. *Music. The Keynote of Human Evolution.* Santa Barbara: J. F. Rowny Press, 1965.

_____. *The Cosmic Harp.* La Canada, CA: New Age Press, 1969.

_____. *The Esoteric Music of Richard Wagner.* La Canada: New Age Press, 1974.

_____. *Color and Music in the New Age.* Los Angeles: New Age Press, 1977.

_____. *Healing and Regeneration Through Music.* Los Angeles: New Age Press, 1978.

_____. *Healing and Regeneration Through Color.* Los Angeles: New Age Press, 1979.

Hodson, Geoffrey. *Music Forms.* Wheaton: Theosophical Press, 1976.

_____. *The Brotherhood of Angels and of Men.* Wheaton: Theosophical Press, 1973.

Holmes, John L. *Conductors on Record.* London: Gollancz, 1982.

Hurd, Michael. *The Orchestra.* New York: Quarto Pub. Co., 1980.

Ismael, Cristina. *The Healing Environment.* Millbrae, CA: Celestial Arts, 1976.

Johnson, James. *Freedom from Depression.* New York: Logos International, 1982.

Johnston, William. *Silent Music.* New York: Harper & Row, 1974.

Keyes, Laurel. *Toning.* Santa Monica: DeVorss & Co., 1973.

Khan, Sufi Inayat. *The Mysticism of Sound.* Netherlands: Servire BV, 1979.

Leonard, Richard Anthony. *The Stream of Music.* Garden City: Dolphin-Doubleday, 1962.

Lewis, Richard, (ed.). *In Praise of Music.* New York: Orion Press, 1963.

Menuhin, Yehudi, & Davis, Curtis. *The Music of Man.* Sydney, Australia: Methuen, 1979.

Munch, Charles. *I Am a Conductor.* New York: Oxford University Press, 1955.

Murchie, Guy. *The Seven Mysteries of Life.* Boston: Houghton Mifflin Co., 1978.

Nette, Paul. *Book of Musical Documents.* New York: Philosophical Library, 1948.

Newhouse, Flower A.. *Speak the Word.* Vista, CA: The Christward Ministry, 1942.

_____. *Insights Into Reality*. (Ed. Stephen and Phyllis Isaac). Escondido, CA: The Christward Ministry, 1975.

_____. *The Kingdom of the Shining Ones*. Escondido, CA: The Christward Ministry, 1955, 1975.

_____. *The Journey Upward*. Escondido, CA: The Christward Ministry, 1978.

_____. *Rediscovering the Angels*. Escondido, CA: The Christward Ministry, 1976.

Ortmans, Kay. *Reminders from Well-Springs*. Ben Lomond, CA: Well-Springs Foundation, 1969.

Podolsky, Edward. *The Doctor Prescribes Music*. New York: Frederick A. Stokes Co., 1939.

Previn, André, ed. *Orchestra*. London: MacDonald & Jane's, 1979.

Rainbow Book, The. Berkeley: Shambhala, 1975.

Ralph, W. Arthur. *The Messiah—A Spiritual Interpretation*. Great Britain: Arthur Stockwell, Ltd., 1980.

Retallack, Dorothy. *The Sound of Music and Plants*. Santa Monica: DeVorss & Co., 1973.

Rosicrucian Fellowship. *The Musical Scale*. Oceanside, CA, 1949.

Roustit, Albert. *Prophecy in Music*. Albert Roustit, 1972.

Salter, Lionel. *The Illustrated Encyclopedia of Classical Music*. London: Salamander Books, 1978.

Schafer, R. Murray. *The Tuning of the World*. New York: Alfred Knopf, 1977.

Scott, Cyril. *Music—Its Secret Influence Throughout the Ages*. New York: Samuel Weiser, Inc., 1969.

Stebbing, Lionel. *Music, Its Occult Basis and Healing Value*. E. Grinstead, Sussex, England: New Knowledge Books, 1961.

Stevenson, Victor, ed. *The Music Makers*. Middlesex, England: Harry Abrams, Inc., 1979.

Sullivan, J. W. M. *Beethoven, His Spiritual Development*. New York: Vintage, 1955.

Teilhard de Chardin, Pierre. *Hymn of the Universe*. New York: Harper & Row, 1965.

_____. *Prayer of the Universe*. New York: Harper & Row, 1965.

_____. *The Heart of Matter*. New York: Harvest Pub., 1978.

Thompson, Oscar. *How to Understand Music and Enjoy It*. New York: Premier-Fawcett, 1958.

Tompkins, Peter. *The Secret Life of Plants*. New York: Avon, 1973.

Van der Leeuw, Gerardus. *Sacred and Profane Beauty in Art*. New York: Abingdon Press, 1965.

Walter, Bruno. *Of Music and Music-Making*. New York: W. W. Norton & Co., 1957.

Index

America, North, nature music of, 88-91

America, South, and Spain, nature music of, 95

Anatomy of an Illness. See Cousins, Norman

Angels: in healing, 100; in music, 87, 91, 99-105, 119, 121, 126, 136, 142; poetic reference to, 9; at weddings, 80

Anger, 21-22, 23-24, 24-25, 53. *See also* Tension; Emotional nature; Temperament

Anxiety. *See* Tensions

Art of Loving, The. See Fromm, Erich

Astrological signs: composers grouped by, 114-38 *passim*; relation to four elements, 39

Author, musical background of, 54-56

Bach, Johann Sebastian, 51, 103, 107, 119-20, 141

Barber, Samuel, 90

Bartok, Bela, 134

Beatles, The, music of, 58

Beethoven, Ludwig van, 88, 95, 101, 107, 121-22, 141

Berlioz, Hector, 56, 94, 101, 112-13, 141

Bernstein, Leonard, 140-41

Bible: astral projection in, 63; music in, 2

Birth and music for, 82

Bizet, Georges, 51, 137-38

Bohm, Georg, 102

Boredom, music to relieve, 29

Brigadoon, 19

Broadway shows, songs from, 20

Brahms, Johannes, 96, 101, 109, 125

Brotherhood, 73, 90, 122

Bruch, Max, 127

Bruckner, Anton, 96, 103, 107, 131-32

Butterworth, George, 92

Cash, Johnny, 19, 26-27

Catalogs, record, 6, 7

Chants, Gregorian, 115-17

Chopin, Frederic, 51, 102, 123-24, 129, 143

Children: introduction of orchestra to, 76-79; music for, 68-81, music of other lands for, 73-76; music to release energy of, 72-73

Christ, music to, 106-13 *passim*; specific selections, 111-12

Closure, 52-53

Color in sound, 139-44 *passim*

Composers, great, 114-38; listed
  by elements: Fire, 133-35;
  Earth, 135-36; Air, 136-37;
  Water, 137-38; Nature com-
  posers, 87-98, 129, 130, 133,
  134, 135, 136
Courage (strength), 6, 29-31, 122
Cousins, Norman, 84
Creativity, 6, 43, 61, 146

Daily life, music for, 62-67
Dances, 18, 20
Death. See Transition
Debussy, Achille Claude, 23, 47,
  94, 132-33, 142
DeFalla, Manuel, 135
Delibes, Leo, 137
Delius, Frederick, 56, 88-89,
  92-93, 99, 130, 138
Depression (fear), 28-29, 119,
  120; rock contributes to, 57
Diamond, Dr. John, 3-4, 12,
  57-58, 70
D'Indy, Vincent, 94, 127, 134
Disney, Walt, 139-40
Divine Presence. See God
Doctor Prescribes Music, The.
  See Podolsky, Dr. Edward
Dvořák, Antonin, 71, 97-98,
  107, 127-28

Eating, music while, 64-66, 118;
  music to curb excessive, 30
Elements, four, 38-46; composers grouped by, 114-38;
  music of each: Fire, 40-41;
  Earth, 42; Air, 43-44; Water,
  45-46; relation to astrology,
  39. See also Temperament
Elgar, Sir Edward, 15-16, 93, 141
Emotional nature (moods): key
  to healthy, 21; instruments

affecting, 14; lifting of, 15,
  16; music for, 20, 21, 21-33,
  130-31, 135, 137-38, 147. See
  also Anger; Depression
  (fear); Temperament; Tensions (anxiety)
England, Scotland, and Wales,
  nature music of, 91-93
Equipment, sound, 11-12

Fairies. See Nature spirits
Fanfares, 18
Fantasia, 139-40
Fatigue: removal of, 5, 15;
  sounds which cause, 58. See
  also Physical body, energiz-
  ing of
Fear. See Depression
Feldenkrais, Moshe, 51
Finzi, Gerald, 92
Fox, Virgil, 55-56
France, nature music of, 93-94
Franck, César, 102, 108, 126-27,
  143
Friends, sharing music with,
  46-47
Fromm, Erich 31
Future, music for, 145-48

Germany and Austria, nature
  music of, 95-96
Glazunov, Alexander, 135
Gluck, Christoph Wilibald, 101,
  120
Goals, daily, 64
God (Divine Presence; Spirit);
  attunement with, 1, 5, 6, 34,
  117; devotion to, 45;
  guidance of, 35, 52, 66; hosts
  of, 34; music as gateway to,
  56, 86; music to, 106-13, 118,
  119, 126, 131; specific
  musical selections to, 111-12

Gounod, 104, 142
Grieg, Edvard, 63, 97, 101, 114, 128-29, 142-43
Guilt, release of, 53

Habits, changing, 51
Hammerstein, 104. *See also* Rodgers and Hammerstein
Handel, George Frideric, 100, 102, 105, 108-9, 118-19
Hanson, Howard, 89
Harmful music, 50, 57-60, 126, 129. *See also* Noise; Overexposure to music; Rock
Harris, Roy, 89
Haydn, Franz Joseph, 51, 71, 72, 120-21, 146
Healing: defined, 4; historical use of music in, 2-3; future use of music in, 147; music for, 13-37, 84-85, 115, 132-33. *See also* Therapy, music as
Heline, Corinne, 106-7, 142
Herbert, Victor, 142
Hodson, Geoffrey, 86-87, 99, 140
Holst, Gustave, 137
Home and family, music for, 25, 68-85
Horn, Paul, 103
Horowitz, Vladimir, 26, 27
Hovhaness, Alan, 38, 90
Humor in music, 84-85, 89, 93, 125
Humperdinck, Englebert, 102, 143
Hymns, 104
Hyperactivity, music for, 28

I Am a Conductor. See Munch, Charles

Imagination, stimulating, 71-72
Insomnia, 66-67
Ives, Charles, 89-90, 136

Johnson, Dr. James E., 57
Journal, musical, 53-54

Listening: enhancement of, 10-12, 50, 71; places for, 11, 25, 48; preparation for, 9-10
Liszt, Franz, 124, 141
Lowen, Alexander, 51
Love and devotion, 31-33; music for, 32

MacDowell, Edward, 88, 136
Mahler, Gustav, 96, 102, 109, 130-31, 141
Marches, 15
Massanet, Jules, 135
Meditation with music, 34-37; musical selections for, 35; preparation for, 35-36
Melody, 13-14, 33, 60, 117
Mendelssohn, 103, 123, 129
Mental nature, 5, 33-34, 135, 137
Moods. *See* Emotional nature
Mozart, Wolfgang, 101, 107, 121
Munch, Charles, 47
Music: defined, 1; deeper mysteries of, 139-44; early, 115-17; types of, 69-70
Music, Its Secret Influence Through the Ages. See Scott, Cyril
Mussorgsky, Modest, 134

Nations: music of (for children), 73-76; nature music of, 88-98

Nature: attunement to, 86-87, 129; music, composers of, 87-98, 128, 130, 135, 136; sounds of, 11, 49

Nature spirits (fairies), 92, 93, 94, 96, 98, 128, 132

Nelson, John, 110

Newhouse, Reverend Flower, 9, 83-84, 86, 99-100; clairvoyant vision of 140, 141-44

Nin, Anais, 49

Noise, 1, 50, 145. See also Harmful music; Rock; Sound

Nursing homes, music in, 3, 16, 51, 117

"Oh, What a Beautiful Morning," 19

Overexposure to music, 15, 17, 18, 19, 77, 126, 129

Overtures, 17-18

Ozawa, Seiji, 32, 55

Past, releasing, 52-53

Physical body: energizing of, 15, 16, 17, 18-19, 77; instruments affecting, 14; music for, 14-20. See also Fatigue; Healing; Therapy, music as

Pictorial music. See Visualization, music for

Podolsky, Dr. Edward, 64-65

Prophecy in Music. See Roustit, Albert

Rachmaninoff, Sergei, 23, 27, 51, 134, 143

Ravel, Maurice, 94, 137

Recordings, digital, 12

Relationships: deepening of, 6, 122, 146; improving, 30, 53; temperament expansion through, 46

Relaxation, music for, 31

Respighi, Ottorino, 103, 137

Rimsky-Korsakov, 98, 138

Rochberg, George, 110

Rock music, 57-58, 60, 70-71, 145. See also Harmful music; Noise

Rodgers and Hammerstein, 63, 90-91, 147. See also Hammerstein

Roustit, Albert, 59

Rubenstein, Artur, 25-26

Russia and Slavic nations, nature music of, 97-98

Scandinavia, nature music of, 96-97

Schubert, Franz, 103, 122-23, 142

Schumann, Robert, 96, 124-25

Scott, Cyril, 136

Scriabin, Alexander, 98, 135, 136, 139

Sibelius, Jan, 60, 97, 128, 135, 142

Songs, lively, 19-20

Soul, music for, 14

Sound: destructive, 60; entering into, 49-50; types of 56-57. See also Harmful music; Music; Nature, sounds of; Noise

Sound of Music, The. See Rodgers and Hammerstein

Soundtracks, 18, 19-20, 146-47

Spirit. See God

Stokowski, Leopold, 17, 139-40

Strength. See Courage

Strauss, Richard, 96, 136

Sullivan, Arthur, 135
Synesthesia, 139-44 *passim*;
    defined, 139

Tastes, musical, 37, 114
Tchaikovsky, Peter, 17, 98,
    129-30, 141
Teilhard de Chardin, Pierre,
    106, 113
Telemann, Georg Philipp, 63,
    118
Temperament, 46-47; elements
    in relation to: Fire, 39-41;
    Earth, 41-42; Air, 42-44;
    Water, 44-46. *See also*
    Elements, four; Emotional
    nature
Tensions (anxiety): music for,
    13-14, 22-23, 118, 123; relief
    of, 5, 27-28

Therapy, music as, 4, 5-6, 12,
    102. *See also* Healing
Transition (death), 83-84

Vaughan Williams, Ralph, 13,
    91-92, 102, 108, 133
Verdi, Giuseppe, 16-17
Villa-Lobos, Heitor, 95, 138
Visualization, 47-49, 71-72;
    music for, 48-49
Vivaldi, Antonio, 63, 117-18
von Suppé, Franz, 134

Wagner, Richard, 47, 96, 101,
    102-3, 107, 125-26, 128
Waking up, music for, 63
Weddings and music for, 79-81

Your Body Doesn't Lie. See Dia-
    mond, Dr. John

Self-help books from Quest

Art of Inner Listening — *By Jessie Crum*
"So you would like to be a genius," writes the author. Simply stop talking — and listen — really listen.

The Choicemaker — *By E.B. Howes & S. Moon*
Man and his intrinsic need to make choices.

Concentration — *By Ernest Wood*
Will help you take full charge of your mind.

Do You See What I See? — *By Jae Jah Noh*
How to live fully, indeed passionately, with no inner conflicts.

Mastering the Problems of Living — *By Haridas Chaudhuri*
Overcome depression! Conquer anxiety! Make decisions!

The Path of Healing — *By H.K. Challoner*
Based on the holistic nature of all life. Heal yourself with harmonious living.

A Way to Self-Discovery — *By I.K. Taimni*
A way of life book for serious students of the "ancient wisdom."

Available from:
The Theosophical Publishing House
306 West Geneva Road, Wheaton, Illinois 60187